VISUAL QUICKSTART GUIDE

iMOVIE '08 & iDVD '08

FOR MAC OS X

Jeff Carlson

Peachpit Press

Visual QuickStart Guide
iMovie '08 & iDVD '08 for Mac OS X
Jeff Carlson

Peachpit Press
1249 Eighth Street
Berkeley, CA 94710
(510) 524-2178
(510) 524-2221 (fax)

Find us on the Web at: www.peachpit.com
To report errors, please send a note to errata@peachpit.com
Peachpit Press is a division of Pearson Education

Editor: Nancy Davis
Production Coordinator: Lisa Brazieal
Composition: Jeff Carlson
Copyediting: Liane Thomas
Proofreading: Tracy O'Connell
Illustrations and photos: Jeff Tolbert, Laurence Chen, Jeff Carlson
Indexer: Ann Rogers

ISBN-13: 978-0-321-50187-5
ISBN-10:   0-321-50187-X

9 8 7 6 5 4 3 2 1

Printed and bound in the United States of America

Dedications:

To Leonard, whose one-month film class at Whitworth instilled in me an appreciation of movies beyond mere popcorn entertainment.

To my sister Lisa, ever encouraging and cheerful.

Special Thanks to:

Nancy Davis, for knowing when to ask, "How are you doing?" and making the author's end of producing a book much easier.

Liane Thomas, for not hesitating to jump into the project when asked, and for her razor-sharp editing eyes.

Ann Rogers, for not only delivering a top-notch index but also sending little encouraging notes as we went along.

Lisa Brazieal, for answering my little production questions, making the final files look beautiful, and for frequently popping up in iChat to say hi.

Laurence Chen and **Gena Morgan,** who provided the photos for the lighting examples in Chapter 4.

Jeff Tolbert, for updating my embarassing line drawings of computer and video equipment, and for creating the lighting renderings in Chapter 4.

Don Sellers, for getting me up to speed with shooting, lighting, sound, composition, and providing a real-world reference.

Derick Mains, Paul Towner, Keri Walker, Janette Barrios, Khyati Shah, and **Theresa Weaver** at Apple for answering my questions and providing resources when I needed them.

The folks at the **University Village Apple Store** for providing answers, assistance, and letting me test some things on their equipment.

The staff at the **University Village Sony Style Store** for answering questions and letting me demo their high-definition camcorders.

Glenn Fleishman, Kim Ricketts, Weston Clay and **Deb Crawford** (plus the various **long-distance inhabitants from earlier office incarnations**) at the Fremont nook for being the best reasons to go to the office every day (well, nearly every day). They're good inspiration and reassurance that this freelance thing actually works.

Nancy Aldrich-Ruenzel, Gary-Paul Prince, and even some non-hyphenated folks like **Cliff Colby, Sara Jane Todd, Scott Cowlin,** and **Paula Baker** at Peachpit Press.

And, of course, **Kim Carlson,** who never hesitates to ask, "How can I help?" and keeps me inspired to do what I do each day (and who wrangles a garden into beautiful submission better than anyone I know).

TABLE OF CONTENTS

INTRODUCTION

The Great iMovie Schism of 2007

In August 2007, Steve Jobs announced iLife '08 by saying that one application was completely new. Instead of a different iApplication, however, the "new" program turned out to be iMovie. Apple believed that iMovie HD was still too complicated for many users, so it tossed out the old and completely rewrote a new application, which we know as iMovie '08.

For longtime iMovie users, the switch has been difficult. Many features they'd grown accustomed to, such as creating DVD chapter markers, are gone. So, too, is support for third-party plug-ins, and any semblance of the old familiar timeline. iMovie '08 is a bold attempt to redefine how regular people edit video, taking its cues from iPhoto instead of Final Cut Pro.

Is it successful? I'm torn. It is possible to make a good movie in less time, which is clearly one of its main goals. And in my testing, I've discovered that what I at first called "iMovie Lite" is a much deeper program. But I'm hoping subsequent revisions will bring back some of the great features that have vanished for now.

I was at Macworld Expo when Apple introduced the first version of iMovie, and seeing it in person was a bona fide "a-ha" moment for me and most of the people in attendance. Video editing, a skill that people spend years mastering in specialized schools, had arrived on the average user's Mac. *Of course* this was going to work. When Steve Jobs presented a short video of two children playing, I knew the days of long, choppy, unedited videotape recordings were coming to a close. Not only can you easily—let me repeat that: *easily*—capture video footage and transfer it to your computer, you can now edit out all the bad shots, the awkward moments, and those times when the camera was inadvertently left recording while dangling at your side.

Now, in late 2007, Apple has helped redefine the whole notion of home movies. With built-in support for the high-definition HDV video format (as well as widescreen digital video and native MPEG-4 formats), iMovie '08 gives you the chops to make your own independent feature film without appearing as if you made it in your basement—even if that's exactly what you did.

And when you're done editing the movie, send it to iDVD '08 to create a professional-looking DVD that can play on most home DVD players. Your friends and family will be the ones saying, "A-ha!"

Who Should Read this Book

iMovie '08 & iDVD '08 for Mac OS X: Visual QuickStart Guide is aimed at the beginning or intermediate videographer who wants to know how to edit movies quickly and easily in iMovie and create DVDs using iDVD. Perhaps you've just purchased your first camcorder and want to turn your home movies into little masterpieces, but don't have the time or money to invest in a professional video editing application. Or maybe you're an old hand at shooting video but new to editing the footage on a computer. Then again, maybe you're a budding Spielberg with scripts in your head and a passion for telling stories on film—the movie business is a tough one to crack, but it's entirely possible that your iMovie-edited film could be the springboard for a career in Hollywood. (In fact, one of the official entries at the 2004 Sundance Film Festival was edited in iMovie.) Or you could also be the owner of a new Mac, and want to know why Apple is going to the trouble of giving you a powerful video editing application *for free*.

Since iMovie's introduction, we've seen a boom in digital video editing. Sure, it was possible before, using much more complicated and expensive programs such as Final Cut Pro or Adobe After Effects (and you can still take that route). But with iMovie and iDVD, *anyone* can make a movie and burn it to a disc that can be played in nearly any consumer DVD player.

What's New in this Edition

With Apple's surprise announcement that iMovie '08 is a completely new program from earlier versions of iMovie, I've almost completely rewritten the iMovie section. The iDVD section has also been updated to account for the changes in the program.

A new chapter, "Make a Movie in a Hurry," gives you the basics for going from captured film to shared movie. I've also created a new chapter called "Managing Video" to account for all the ways in which iMovie handles and stores footage.

An iMovie and iDVD Toolbox

A full-size movie crew can be unbelievably large and take up a city block. You probably won't require that much gear, but a few items are necessary to use iMovie and iDVD.

- ◆ **Mac OS X 10.4.9 or later.** iMovie '08 and iDVD '08 run under Apple's now and future operating system, Mac OS X, version 10.4.9 or later (including Mac OS X 10.5 Leopard). You also need a Mac with an Intel processor, a Power Mac G5 (dual 2.0 GHz or faster), or iMac G5 (1.9 GHz or faster).

- ◆ **iMovie '08 and iDVD '08.** If you've purchased a Mac sometime after August 2007, you probably have iMovie and iDVD already—look in the folder named *Applications*. The programs are also available as part of the $80 iLife '08 package, which includes iPhoto '08, GarageBand '08, and iWeb '08.

- ◆ **A digital camcorder.** This handy and compact device records the raw footage you will edit in iMovie. If you own a camcorder that's not digital, you can still import video into iMovie using a third-party analog-to-digital converter. That said, I can't stress how much easier it is to work when you have a digital camcorder.

- ◆ **Lots of hard disk space.** Storage is getting cheaper by the day, which is a good thing. You'll need lots. I don't mean a few hundred megabytes tucked away in a corner of your drive. Realistically, if you don't have at least 10 GB (gigabytes) of storage (on the low side) to use for iMovie and iDVD, shop for a bigger hard drive.

The Moviemaking Process

Creating a movie can be a huge spectrum of experience, but for our purposes I'm going to distill it as follows.

1. **Preproduction.** If you're filming a scripted movie (with actors, sets, dialogue, etc.), be sure you hire the actors, build the sets, write the script, and otherwise prepare to shoot a film. See Appendix B for some resources on where to learn more about the process of getting a movie before the cameras. On the other hand, if you're shooting an event or vacation, preproduction may entail making sure you have a camcorder (see Chapter 1), its batteries are charged, and that you have enough tape available.

2. **Capture footage.** With preproduction out of the way, it's time to actually film your movie. The shooting part is when this book starts to come in handy. Chapters 2 through 5 discuss methods of composing your shots, lighting the scenes, and capturing audio.

3. **Import footage into iMovie.** Your tape is full of raw video waiting to be sculpted by your keen eye and innate sense of drama. The next step is importing it onto your computer and into iMovie. See Chapter 8.

4. **Edit your footage in iMovie.** Before iMovie, average folks had no simple way to edit their footage. The result was endless hours of suffering as relatives were forced to watch every outtake, flubbed shot, and those 10 minutes of walking when you thought the camera was turned off. iMovie changes all that. See Chapter 6 for a quick overview, and then delve into Chapters 7 through 13 to learn how to edit your video and audio, plus add elements such as transitions and titles.

5. **Export video.** The movie is complete, and it's a gem. Now you need to share it with the world. Using the information found in Chapters 14 through 16, you can share it with other Apple programs and devices such as the iPod and Apple TV, upload it to the Web, or export it to a QuickTime movie for downloading or further manipulation.

The DVD Creation Process

iDVD provides a clear path to customizing the appearance of your DVD, adding more content, and burning the DVD disc.

1. **Choose a theme.** iDVD's professionally designed themes provide a menu system that your viewers interact with to watch your movie. Chapter 18 shows you how to expand the menu's organization by adding submenus and AutoPlay movies.

2. **Customize themes and add more content.** With the bare bones in place, change the theme's settings to personalize the menus. Learn how to change buttons, replace background images, modify text formatting, build slideshows, and more in Chapters 20 and 21.

3. **Burn, baby, burn!** Choose an encoding method and burn your disc, or create a project archive that can be moved to another computer for burning there (such as a faster Mac). The smoke rises over Chapter 22.

This Book's Companion Web Site

I maintain a frequently updated iMovie blog that includes additional tips, pointers to software, examples from the book, and other iLife-related information. Check often at http://www.jeffcarlson.com/imovievqs/.

What You Can Accomplish by the End of this Book

To say, "Prepare your acceptance speech" would be exaggerating a bit, but theoretically, you can use iMovie to create a feature film, award-winning documentary, or even just the best darn vacation video you've ever seen. As you delve deeper into digital video and nonlinear editing (NLE), you'll realize that more options and more control can be had with more sophisticated (and pricey) systems, such as Final Cut Express and Final Cut Pro. But nothing says you can't do what you want with iMovie.

Stepping out of the clouds, you should easily (there's that word again) be able to shoot, edit, and distribute your movie. In the process, you'll find a new respect for film and video—you can't help it. After using iMovie for a few hours, you'll start watching television with a new eye that picks up aspects like pacing, framing, transitions, and audio you may never have noticed before.

That's been my experience, and now look at me: I've written six editions of this book. And assembled some of the best darn vacation movies you've ever seen.

Part 1
Shooting

THE DIGITAL CAMCORDER

Ages ago, my copy of iMovie 1.0 sat neglected on my hard drive for months because I had no easy way to import video footage. I could have used an analog-to-digital converter to bring in the contents of old videotapes (see Chapter 8), but it would have been a hassle. What I needed was a digital camcorder.

Although digital camcorders cost more than analog models, you can get a good quality model these days for less than $400. You can also easily spend $5,000 or more, with plenty of models falling between those ranges.

iMovie '08 gives you another option: high-definition (HD) digital camcorders that capture video at a much higher resolution. You can get one for around $900 currently, a bargain compared to full-fledged HD systems (more on that topic in this chapter).

For the money, you also get a host of features—and gimmicks. If you've not yet purchased a digital camcorder, this chapter will help you decide which combination of features is right for you. Note that I'll give some examples, but won't be recommending any particular model because (like all technology) the field changes pretty quickly. If you already own a camcorder, skim this chapter to see which features are important and which you should turn off.

Buying a Camcorder

If you don't yet own a digital camcorder, you need one. Here's a look at the important characteristics of these devices.

HD or DV format

iMovie offers you an important choice: should you shoot in standard DV (digital video, also sometimes referred to as SD, or standard definition), or in HD (high-definition video)?

Prior to 2004, shooting in HD required expensive cameras costing tens or hundreds of thousands of dollars. Now, you can get an HD camcorder for less than $900 (**Figure 1.1**).

HD video captures more image information than standard DV, and comes in two variations (**Figure 1.2**): *720p* measures 1,280 by 720 pixels, and captures each frame in its entirety (known as "progressive" capture, the "p" in 720p); *1080i* measures 1,920 by 1,080 pixels, and interlaces each frame (hence the "i"; see **Figure 1.3**). HD also shoots in a 16:9 widescreen aspect ratio. As you might expect, video shot with HD cameras looks great on an HD television.

iMovie supports two high-definition formats that are designed to minimize the data rate and work on consumer hardware: HDV (High Definition Video) is a consumer-level version of HD that uses MPEG-2 compression; AVCHD (Advanced Video Codec High Definition) uses MPEG-4 compression and stores footage on removable memory cards or an internal hard drive on some models. For example, you can connect an HDV camera to your Mac using a FireWire cable and import the footage onto regular hard drives. By comparison, working with uncompressed 10-bit HD video requires massive amounts of storage, around 500 GB per hour of footage (see Chapter 8 for HD storage requirements).

Figure 1.1 Panasonic's HDC-SD1 high-definition camcorder costs less than $900 (street price), a sign that HD prices are finally coming down.

DV: 720 by 480 pixels

HD 720p: 1,280 by 720 pixels

HD 1080i: 1,920 by 1,080 pixels

Figure 1.2 HD uses much more image information than standard DV video. Also note that HD features a 16:9 widescreen aspect ratio, while SD uses the television standard 4:3 ratio.

Progressive frame

Interlaced frame   *Next interlaced frame*

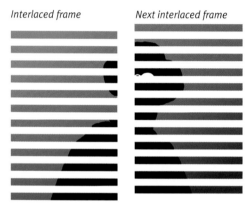

Figure 1.3 A progressive frame is captured in its entirety, the way each frame of film is recorded. Interlaced video captures every other line (exaggerated here for clarity) so that as the frames are played back, your eye sees the image as a solid picture. Interlacing can capture larger images because it's actually storing about half of the image information for each frame. (Interlacing is also the way most televisions operate.)

So although you're not getting the same super-high quality as someone shooting with a $200,000 setup, you still end up with beautiful HD footage.

✔ Tips

- iDVD handles incoming HD video, but it can't currently burn the HD-quality version to a DVD. Two competing high-definition DVD formats are jostling for position in the entertainment and computer industries: HD-DVD and Blu-Ray DVD, each backed by major corporate entities. Considering that the Hollywood movie studios now make more money from DVD sales than from theatrical screenings, it's a hotly contested fight for dominance. Apple is on the board of Blu-Ray, so it's likely (but not guaranteed) that the SuperDrives in future Macs will be capable of burning HD video to Blu-Ray discs. But until the discs begin appearing, iDVD compresses the HD video to make it fit onto today's DVD media.

- You need an Intel-based Mac to work with AVCHD footage.

- Camcorders that record to DVD using the AVCHD format are not supported in iMovie '08. For more on camera compatibility, go to `apple.com/support/imovie`.

- To edit HD in its native resolution, you need a computer monitor at least 23 inches in size, such as Apple's Cinema HD Displays.

- The full scope of HD video production is enough to fill several books. For hands-on, in-the-trenches coverage of HD, I turn to Mike Curtis's *HD for Indies* weblog (`www.hdforindies.com`). Also check out *FresHDV* (`www.freshdv.com`), and the companion Web site for this book (`jeffcarlson.com/imovie/`).

BUYING A CAMCORDER

MiniDV tape format

To capture the best quality footage, get a camcorder that uses the MiniDV format (**Figure 1.4**). MiniDV tapes are compact, store 100 percent digital information, and record between 60 minutes (at standard playing, or SP, speed) or 90 minutes (at long playing, or LP, speed) of footage. They're not particularly cheap, but they're not too expensive either. An online search shows you can find them in bulk for around $3 to $5 per cassette.

MiniDV can store roughly 500 horizontal lines of resolution, which means you're capturing more information than other formats (televisions display about 330 lines). It can also record 16-bit audio at 48 kHz, which is slightly better than CD-quality. What's more, MiniDV tapes retain that quality when you record over them, or make copies from other MiniDV tapes.

Tapeless camcorders

To make cameras even smaller, manufacturers are avoiding tape altogether and releasing cameras that store footage on flash memory (usually CompactFlash or SD cards, the type found in digital still cameras), smaller-sized DVD discs, and built-in hard drives. In fact, some still cameras feature movie modes that shoot nearly as well as a dedicated camcorder. iMovie can import this footage (see Chapter 8), but the data is shrunk using MPEG-4 compression, which degrades the image quality.

✔ Tip

■ It doesn't seem to matter which brand of MiniDV tape you choose—only that you stick with the same one. Companies use different lubricants on their tapes, so mixing brands can potentially lead to a sticky, camera-damaging mess.

Figure 1.4 As part of the miniaturization of digital camcorders, the tape media is smaller, too. But despite the size, MiniDV tapes store roughly one hour of high-quality video. HDV camcorders use the same tapes and store the same amount of footage.

Why Image Quality Is No Longer the Most Important Feature

Recording to tape provides the best image quality for SD video (HDV is written to tape, but stored as compressed MPEG-2 video). And yet, tapeless camcorders are selling in far greater numbers, despite the fact that those camcorders compress the footage and offer reduced image quality. Why the switch?

Convenience. Tape is linear, so you can't just jump to a particular scene without fast-forwarding or rewinding. It also requires that you import the footage in real time, making you wait an hour (for a typical full tape) before you can do any editing. As a result, a lot of tape ends up stacked on shelves or buried in drawers. For most people, it appears, the quality loss with tapeless formats is an acceptable trade-off.

I still subscribe to the notion that you want to start with the highest-quality image you can, but as the performance of AVCHD and other formats improves, I may end up changing my mind.

Figure 1.5 Today's digital camcorders are small enough to fit in your palm.

NTSC or PAL

Standard-definition video is broadcast in one of two formats, depending on where you live. In the Americas and many Asian countries, the standard is NTSC (National Television Systems Committee), which runs at 30 frames per second (actually 29.97 fps). In several European and some Asian countries, the standard is PAL (Phase Alternating Line), which runs at 25 fps. In most cases, you don't need to choose one or the other—you get whatever is predominant in your area. However, some people prefer to shoot in PAL because it's closer to the film projection rate of 24 fps. Either way, iMovie automatically detects the type of camera that is connected and adjusts its settings to accommodate.

Camcorder size

Ah, camcorder envy. You're carrying a new, tiny, handheld camcorder, but then you spy someone whose camcorder is even more compact. For those of us who've lugged shoulder-mounted VHS cameras back in the day, the miniaturization of camcorder technology is amazing. Although the majority of digital camcorders aren't super small, they're remarkable nonetheless—many fit into a large pants pocket or small purse (**Figure 1.5**).

The small sizes are ultra convenient, but have two drawbacks. You're paying a premium for compactness, so expect to shell out more money for a smaller device. Also, a small camcorder that doesn't weigh much can be harder to keep steady when shooting. If you're looking for something portable to use for grabbing footage anywhere and anytime, go as small as you can afford. If you anticipate more staged shots, where a camera can sit on a tripod for hours, size becomes less of an issue.

Charge-coupled device (CCD)

A traditional movie camera records light onto a strip of film as it passes through the lens. In a digital camcorder, the light comes through the lens and is recorded by a charge-coupled device (CCD), containing arrays of thousands or millions of tiny sensors that note the color of light striking them. When you put the sensors all together, they create the image you see on video.

Most camcorders come with a single CCD, varying in size and resolution. In general, more resolution is better, even though video output is the same—you're paying for better image fidelity, not necessarily a higher number of pixels, as with digital still cameras.

FireWire/i.Link and USB

As you'll soon discover, digital video data is massive, occupying about 3.6 MB *per second* for standard DV footage (see Chapter 8). Even a short movie would take forever to transfer from your camcorder to your Mac if not for the FireWire connection between the two (**Figure 1.6**). Also known on Sony camcorders as i.Link, FireWire is necessary to import movies from SD and HDV cameras into iMovie.

Tapeless camcorders increasingly use USB 2.0 ports, which offer about the same transfer speed as FireWire.

✔ Tips

- Most digital camcorders don't come with a FireWire cable, even though they include a FireWire port. Check the packaging that came with your Mac—Apple includes this cable with some models (**Figure 1.7**).

- If you use a USB hub to connect multiple devices to your Mac, make sure it's capable of USB 2.0 speeds.

FireWire/DV port

Figure 1.6 The 4-pin FireWire port on a digital camcorder is smaller than the one on your Mac.

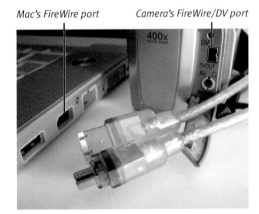

Mac's FireWire port   *Camera's FireWire/DV port*

Figure 1.7 Use a high-speed FireWire connection to import your footage into iMovie on your Mac. You may need to purchase a cable like this one, which has both sizes of FireWire plugs.

Three-CCD Camcorders

Top-of-the-line camcorders feature three separate CCDs, each of which captures a specific color: red, green, or blue. You're not gaining any more image resolution, but the overall color quality is better than that offered by single-CCD cameras. Three-CCD devices tend to cost more, but are coming down in price.

Figure 1.8 Canon's XL H1 is a high-definition MiniDV camera with all the trimmings. The microphone is mounted above the unit to record what you're shooting, not the sound of the camera itself.

Figure 1.9 An LCD viewfinder lets you shoot at odd angles. Rotate the screen to view the shot.

Microphone

Every digital camcorder has a microphone, usually built into the body of the camera, but sometimes mounted to the top or front of the camera (**Figure 1.8**). One thing to watch out for is where the microphone is housed: if it's too close to the camcorder's motors, it could pick up the sound of the camera operating (including the motors used for zoom control). Whenever possible, experiment with a few different camcorder models to check their audio output. You can also attach an external microphone to the camera. See Chapter 5 for more information.

LCD viewfinder

Most digital camcorders include a liquid crystal display (LCD) viewfinder that pops out from the side of the camera and shows you what the lens sees. LCDs vary in size, from 2.5 inches (diagonal) on up. You can use it in place of the built-in viewfinder, which is often advantageous when you need to hold the camera above your head or near your feet (**Figure 1.9**), or if you're filming yourself and want to make sure your head hasn't slipped out of frame. (On some newer camcorders, the LCD is the only way to see what you're shooting.) The LCD is especially useful when you want to review the footage you've taken, or show some video to a few people looking over your shoulder. And you'll find it invaluable for fast-forwarding to the end of your footage to make sure you don't accidentally shoot over your existing video.

✔ Tip

- Remember, it takes power to light up the LCD's pixels and backlighting. Using it often will drain your camera's batteries faster than using the built-in viewfinder. Some cameras now include a switch to turn off or reduce the LCD's backlight to conserve battery power.

Electronic image stabilization

I'll likely spend this entire book saying, "You know what else is great about digital?" So I'll help you get used to it now. Another great thing about a modern digital camcorder is that the software running it can help you stabilize your image and prevent the shaky footage associated with small handheld cameras. To do this, the camcorder uses an outer portion of the total image as reference, then compares movement of objects within the field of view to the outer area (**Figure 1.10**). If most of the image moves together, the software assumes the whole camera is moving instead of just the objects, and compensates by shifting the active image.

Electronic image stabilization is helpful, but certainly has its drawbacks. It doesn't record the entire screen, so in some cases you may find that objects on the periphery don't show up in the final footage. It's also not good if you're intentionally moving the camera, such as when you pan or zoom, because the software has to figure out that your motion is deliberate; the end result is sometimes blurry motion that would otherwise be clearer. Still, compared to footage that looks like it was shot during an earthquake, these trade-offs become more acceptable.

✔ Tip

■ Of course, image stabilization isn't so good that it will make the shot you took while running down the street look like it was filmed with a Steadicam.

Guide area

Image shifted, prompting the camera to compensate

Figure 1.10 In this *massively* simplified diagram, the original image (top) is shifted to the right (bottom) by the camera operator's nervousness around such towering animals. The camera compares the image to the pixels in the unrecorded guide area and compensates by shifting the main image to match. (In reality, the camera doesn't use such a huge guide area—it divides the entire image into several quadrants and continually compares each guide area to its corresponding image area.)

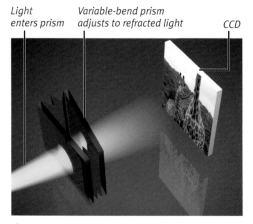

Light enters prism   *Variable-bend prism adjusts to refracted light*   CCD

Figure 1.11 An optical image stabilization system uses two lenses to detect light refraction.

Optical image stabilization

Another option for stabilizing your video is to buy a camera with *optical* image stabilization. Unlike the digital method, optical stabilization uses a prism composed of two lenses with silicon fluid between them. The prism determines whether the light coming into the lens is refracted (think of how a stick poking halfway out of water appears to bend below the water's surface). If it is, the camcorder adjusts the lenses to remove the refraction (**Figure 1.11**). An optical stabilizer can work a bit slower than electronic stabilization—since it's performing mechanical, not digital, adjustments—but tends to be a bit smoother overall.

Lens optics

The camera's lens is your eye to the footage you'll shoot, so optical quality is an important consideration. The lenses in the majority of cameras are of good quality, but more-expensive models tend to feature better optics. I'm not saying more expensive lenses are always better, of course. Research different models and read owner reviews online to learn more.

Remote control

It's not like you don't have enough remote controls lying around the house. I thought having a remote control for a camera was a dumb idea until I realized its two main purposes: playing back video when the camera is attached to a television or monitor, and controlling recording when you can't be near the camera (such as when you're in the frame). The remote ends up being more important than I thought.

BUYING A CAMCORDER

Features Worth Noting

Electronics manufacturers love to make
bulleted lists of features. Some you may
never need or want, while others can help
you improve the footage you shoot.

Focus

It's a safe bet that you want the subjects
in your video to be in focus—but which
subjects, and when? Camcorders feature
automatic focus control, which is great when
you're shooting footage on the fly. Who
wants to try to manually focus when following animals in the wild (**Figure 1.12**)?

However, sometimes the automatic focus
can be too good, bringing most objects in a
scene into focus—which is why camcorders
include an option for manually focusing the
lens. (Higher-end models include a focus
ring built around the lens, like on a 35mm
still camera. Most smaller camcorders sport
small dials or scroll wheels to control manual
focus.) Manual focus is essential for some
situations, such as interviews, when you're
not moving the camera (see Chapter 2).

Shutter speed

The term "shutter speed" is a bit mislead-
ing here, since a digital camcorder doesn't
technically have a shutter (a door or iris
that opens quickly to allow light to enter
the lens). However, it's possible to duplicate
the effects of different shutter speeds by
changing the setting on the camera. This
is good for filming action with movement
that would otherwise appear blurry (such as
sporting events). Shutter speed is measured
in fractions of a second, so a setting of 1/60 is
slower than 1/8000 (see Chapter 3).

Figure 1.12 Gratuitous vacation footage inserted here.
But really, when you're shooting video on the run,
trying to focus manually at the same time would have
meant losing the shot. You can view this movie clip at
this book's companion Web site (jeffcarlson.com/
imovie).

Normal

Low-light setting

Figure 1.13 Some camcorders feature a low-light setting, which boosts the effectiveness of the available light.

Night vision/low light

You have a few options for filming in low-light conditions. You could always carry around a full lighting setup, but that's not realistic. To compensate, some cameras include a night-vision mode that picks up heat from objects near the camera and displays a greenish representation of the scene.

Other cameras may include a low-light setting, which boosts the amount of available light that's picked up by the camera's image sensors (**Figure 1.13**). It's surprisingly effective, though the playback can be stuttered or blurry if a lot of movement is in the scene.

S-Video or HDMI port

All camcorders offer some type of output port so you can hook up a television or monitor to play back your footage. Usually, RCA-style plugs are included, but some models also offer an S-Video port. Hooking up your camera to a TV with an S-Video cable provides a clearer picture than with other AV cables. Use it if you've got it.

Modern high-definition televisions include one or more HDMI (High-Definition Multimedia Interface) ports, which enable you to connect one HDMI cable that transfers both video and audio. Some HD camcorders now include HDMI ports as well.

Features to Ignore/Avoid

Just as there are features you should pay attention to, some features should be ignored or outright avoided. Most of these are included for buyers who don't have the means to edit their movies after shooting. Most importantly, these effects permanently alter your footage, which you can't correct later in iMovie.

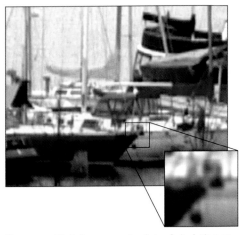

Figure 1.14 Digital zoom creates lots of pixelation as the camera tries to interpolate the image.

♦ **Digital zoom.** One of the first features you'll see on a camera is that it has a 200X (or higher) digital zoom. The technical interpretation is that the computer inside the camera digitally enlarges the image it's seeing, and it appears as if the camera is zoomed beyond its optical capabilities (**Figure 1.14**). The real-world interpretation, at least for now, is that some marketer somewhere is smiling and thinking about the wisdom of P.T. Barnum. Digital zoom isn't pure hokum, but it's also not a mature enough technology to be used in your movies. I expect that as cameras become more powerful and the image processing chips and software speed up (as they inevitably will), digital zoom will become a powerful tool. But not yet.

♦ **Special effects.** Before iMovie, you couldn't apply "sophisticated" techniques such as fade-in or fade-out without using an expensive professional editing system. So, camcorder makers added the capability to apply fades, wipes, and image distortions such as sepia tones or solarization (**Figure 1.15**). Well, forget special effects entirely—you can do them better in iMovie, with more control, and without degrading your footage.

Figure 1.15 In-camera special effects are really only good for ruining otherwise good footage. And not to sound mean, but the Mosaic (top) and Wave (bottom) effects shown here aren't even that interesting.

Date stamp

Figure 1.16 iMovie notes the date and time a clip was shot, so you don't need to use a date stamp feature that permanently adds it to the footage.

◆ **Date stamp.** You can optionally display the date and time on your footage, which would appear to be helpful if not for the fact that the information remains on the tape. Even with this feature disabled, your camcorder is recording (but not displaying) this data, which shows up in iMovie when you view information about a clip (**Figure 1.16**). Similarly, avoid built-in options for adding titles.

◆ **Still photo.** Most cameras now include the capability to take still photos. This is a good idea in theory, but the execution varies widely. Some cameras can capture progressive-scan images—which means every pixel is grabbed—and then save them to a separate memory card (such as SD or Sony Memory Stick cards). These result in better images, depending on the camera, but still not as good as what you'd get from most digital still cameras. A few models now include separate CCDs (and even separate lenses) to take higher quality images.

The technology is always improving, so it's possible that soon you may be able to buy a still photo and video camera combination that works well for both tasks. But personally, I'm more comfortable carrying two cameras that each excels at its appointed tasks.

FEATURES TO IGNORE/AVOID

COMPOSITION AND COVERAGE

Camcorder in hand, it's time to start shooting. Where to start? The easiest route is to point the lens at something and start recording. You're bound to get some good footage. However, by learning how to improve your video as you shoot it, you'll end up with better source footage when it's time to edit.

The material in this chapter (and the rest of the chapters in this section of the book) isn't rocket science. If you've grown up watching television or movies (as we all have, to varying degrees), some of it may be too obvious to warrant mentioning. And yet, when it comes time to shoot, it's all too easy to forget the basics and just let the camcorder run—again, perfectly acceptable, but you might kick yourself when you start working with your footage in iMovie. Remember, with iMovie you can edit your clips into a professional-looking movie, but it can't help you improve mediocre source material.

In this chapter, I'll touch upon the basics of getting a shot, and introduce you to some techniques for framing your scenes and shooting plenty of coverage to work with later. Depending on what you're shooting, some or all of this material may apply—you may have control over aspects such as lighting and how the subjects act, or you may be on safari trying to film elephants while avoiding getting eaten by lions.

Preproduction

In general, the term *preproduction* refers to everything done before the camera starts rolling. I think it's safe to assume that you know how to operate your camcorder, and you probably know roughly what you want to shoot. The following steps—except for the first one, which I consider essential—are optional, depending on the type of movie you're shooting. (For example, feel free to storyboard your baby's first steps, but she'll ultimately be the one to decide how that scene plays out.)

◆ **Imagine the end result.** Before you even turn on your camcorder, think about how the video will be seen. Will it be viewed on a television, movie screen, computer monitor, or maybe a combination of them all? This decision will help you when shooting. For example, if your movie will only appear on the Web, you may want to shoot more close-ups of people, to make sure they're identifiable in a 320 by 160-pixel window on your computer screen. If it's going to be shown on a big-screen television, on the other hand, you could frame your shots with wider vistas or complex background action in the shot.

◆ **Write the script.** If you're shooting a fictional story with scenes, sets, actors, and the like, you're going to need a script. Sure, the bigwigs in Hollywood don't always start movies with a script, but you've no doubt seen one of those stinkers and wondered if entire sections of Los Angeles underwent covert lobotomies. A good movie starts with a good script, without exception. Even in the low-budget world of digital video filmmaking, a good script can often overcome bland direction, lighting, staging, acting, sound, etc.

An Afternoon, A Life

Shortly after starting work on the first edition of this book, I spent an afternoon with a colleague of mine, who also happens to be an Emmy-winning filmmaker, to pick his brain about filmmaking. "Anything in particular?" he asked me.

"Shooting, lighting, sound...," I replied.

He laughed. "Some people spend their entire lives learning just *one* of those skills."

Filmmaking is an evolutionary art, and involves far more than I can include in this book. I'll cover the basics, but I highly recommend consulting Appendix B for resources on where to learn more about shooting.

PREPRODUCTION

- **Create storyboards.** Another step in producing a good fictional movie is creating storyboards: shot-by-shot sketches of what you want to shoot (**Figure 2.1**). In fact, you can use storyboards for documentary-style shooting, too. The point of storyboarding is to formulate your idea of what to shoot before you actually shoot; this process will save you time and help ensure that you're capturing all the visuals you want. At the very least, make a list of things you want to shoot, even if you're grabbing vacation video.

- **Prepare your equipment.** Do you have plenty of MiniDV cassettes or memory cards? Spare batteries—and are they charged? Power cord or battery charger? Lens cleaning cloth? Tripod? "Going to shoot video" can simply mean bringing your body and camcorder; or, it can involve hauling truckloads of equipment. In either case, make sure you have what you'll need to accomplish the job.

Figure 2.1 Drawing up a storyboard will help you visualize your shots and save time. If you're shooting casually or on the go, create a list of shots you want to try to capture. (Your storyboards are likely to run left-to-right, like most, but I'm working in a vertical layout here.)

PREPRODUCTION

Understanding Timecode

Timecode is the measurement system for keeping track of where on a tape or in memory your footage is stored. DV and HDV camcorders use traditional timecode that recognizes individual frames. Many tapeless camcorders refer to the time in just hours, minutes, and seconds. (iMovie '08 uses both formats; see Chapter 10.)

DV and HDV camcorders

As you shoot, you're recording video to the MiniDV tape. If you ever want to find that footage again, you need to understand timecode, the method camcorders use to label and keep track of footage.

As the tape advances, the camcorder notes precise points on the tape where footage is being recorded and displays a numeric tracking code in the viewfinder or on the LCD screen (**Figure 2.2**). A full timecode notation looks like this:

```
01:42:38:12
```

The interpretation of those numbers is a lot like telling time on a digital clock, except for the last two digits:

```
Hours:Minutes:Seconds:Frames
```

So, our timecode number above is read as 1 hour, 42 minutes, 38 seconds, and 12 frames. NTSC digital video records at 30 frames per second (fps), so the last number starts at :00 and ends at :29; for PAL video, which records at 25 fps, the range is between :00 and :24.

When you're recording, you typically won't see all of those numbers. More common is something like 0:03:31 (zero hours, 3 minutes, and 31 seconds), because the camera doesn't split out partial seconds (so no frame numbers are shown).

Timecode indicator

Figure 2.2 The camera assigns a timecode to each frame of film, which is used to manage your footage later in iMovie.

Timecode indicator

Figure 2.3 Some tapeless camcorders count video in hours, minutes, and seconds instead of traditional timecode.

Tapeless camcorders

Tapeless camcorders record each scene as a separate element in memory (whether that's a memory card, DVD, or hard disk), so they don't use timecode. Instead, each clip starts at zero (**Figure 2.3**). (The original capture time is saved, however; in iMovie, choose View > Playhead Info, or press Command-I, to see this label.)

This situation isn't a problem in iMovie, since all clips appear as discreet items whose time markers begin at zero.

Shooting Video Without Disruption

I'm always a little self-conscious when I'm shooting, because often I have to make myself conspicuous in order to get the shot I want. On vacation, this isn't always a problem (my little camcorder is much less intrusive than that other guy's honkin' 35mm lens), but some occasions—for example, weddings—call for discretion. You can take a few different approaches to shooting without disruption.

For one, you don't have to shoot with the camera in front of your face. You can rotate the LCD screen and film from your hip (or even shoot behind you). If it's inevitable that your camera is going to be noticeable, don't be rude about it. People will understand if you need to step softly into view for a few seconds to get a shot, then retreat to a neutral location. Depending on the circumstances, try to ingratiate yourself into the scene so the people involved will trust that you won't be obnoxious.

Or, you could take the route of a professional still photographer who was on a recent vacation I took: Not only was he taking great pictures, he offered to sell the resulting photos to fellow vacationers. People (at least the ones whom I assume bought the album) no longer seemed to mind so much if he blocked their view.

Take Notes

When shooting, you may think you'll remember that the panda bears were located at roughly the 24-minute mark of the Panasonic tape with the purple label, but in reality you'll find yourself scanning through the footage and wishing you'd taken the time to take notes. Get a simple binder and make columns for the tape, timecode, and notes. Then, as you're shooting, jot down what you've just filmed. It doesn't have to be complicated, as long as it offers a quick reference to where your scenes occur. Taking notes is also essential when you need to keep track of locations and the names of people who appear in your video.

✔ Tips

- Label your tapes and memory cards. They add up quickly, tend to look alike, and are guaranteed to fall off your desk in a cluttered heap just before you need to grab the right one in a hurry.

- Listen, I hate taking notes, too. With digital video, however, you have an advantage: Before or after a shot, simply keep the camera running and speak your details. It won't help you find a clip in the middle of a tape, but it will give you the important details of what was recorded.

- Another suggestion is to use a few seconds of your video to record informative signs or other helpful visual indicators (**Figure 2.4**). You don't need to use this footage in your movie, but it helps as a reference when you're editing.

Footage for movie

Footage for reference

Figure 2.4 In lieu of keeping a notebook, take shots of signs or other identifying markers.

Figure 2.5 Sweeping vistas don't always work in small movie windows, so try to shoot large when you can. Don't abandon wide shots, however. Tape is relatively cheap, so grab the shot when it's available; you can intercut the wider shots later when you're editing in iMovie. See "Coverage" later in this chapter.

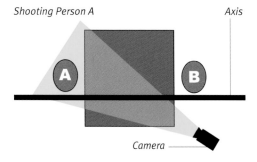

Shooting Person A   Axis

Camera

Shooting Person B

Figure 2.6 Keeping the camera on the same side of your axis line helps the viewer maintain a mental geography of the scene.

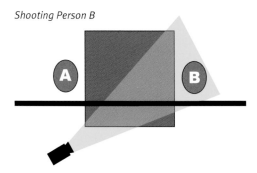

Composing Your Shots

If you really want to, you can hold the camcorder up in the air and hit record—with your eyes closed. But by putting a small amount of thought into the composition of your shots, you can give them a much more professional look.

Shoot large

I had the opportunity to see a 70mm print of *Lawrence of Arabia* a few years ago on the massive screen at Seattle's Cinerama theater. The movie is filled with sweeping desert vistas where you can see miles in every direction, taking full advantage of a large-screen experience.

Most likely, your video will instead play on a television screen or as a QuickTime movie on a Web page (**Figure 2.5**). For that reason, try to "shoot large"—make sure the subject is large enough in the frame that it's instantly recognizable even on a small screen. Getting closer also reveals more detail than can be seen from a distance.

Maintain an axis

Most people are fluent enough in the language of film that they aren't thrown by sudden cuts or changes in a scene. But visually crossing an axis tends to freak them out. The idea is this: if you have two people in a scene, and you're switching between close-ups of each one, they should both remain on their own sides of the screen (**Figure 2.6**). If character A is on the left side of the table, but then you move the camera so that he appears on the right side of the *screen*, the viewer is left wondering how he moved so quickly. At the very least, she'll notice that something odd has happened, which distracts her from the movie's content.

Balance your shots

As I look through still photos I've taken over the years, I notice an annoying consistency: everything is centered. People, monuments, sunsets—all evenly positioned between the edges of the frame. Perhaps it's just our nature to center objects, but it's a good habit to break. Go watch television or a movie and you'll see that almost nothing is centered.

Positioning elements slightly askew of center makes them more interesting. Another take on this positioning is called the *rule of thirds*: the focus of your composition should appear one third of the way from the edge of the frame (**Figure 2.7**). Also make sure that the subject is facing into the frame, not toward the outside (**Figure 2.8**).

✔ Tips

- As you're shooting, be aware of everything in your field of view—don't just focus your attention on the subject. If something else is distracting or disturbing elsewhere in the frame, viewers will likely gravitate toward that, and away from your subject.

- Similarly, take your environment into consideration when possible. Because video is interlaced (every other horizontal line on the television screen is displayed), some objects such as window blinds may create distracting patterns onscreen.

- Many cameras today have the capability to shoot in a 16:9 aspect ratio, also known as widescreen mode. On some cameras, it looks as if the image has been squished in from the sides, but iMovie can interpret the ratio correctly.

Figure 2.7 The train's engine appears in the first third vertical portion of this shot.

Figure 2.8 When your subject faces toward the middle of the frame, he remains engaged with the rest of the shot, rather than looking outside the frame at something else (which is then where your viewers will want to look).

Figure 2.9 Camcorders do a good job of focusing—sometimes too good. In this shot, Greta is competing with the chair and the firepit in the background for the viewer's attention.

Figure 2.10 Objects in the foreground, such as the branches of this tree, can throw off your camcorder's automatic focus and obscure what you wanted to capture (in this case, a rhino in the wild).

Avoid Bouncing Video

If you're shooting a fixed object where the camera won't move (such as a person being interviewed), use manual focus. Sometimes the motion of the person talking (if they move forward slightly when making a point, for example) will trigger the camera to adjust its automatic focus, causing other elements in the frame to "bounce."

Focus

Pity the poor UFO watchers of days gone by, with their bulky cameras and—most distressingly—manual focus. It's hard enough to spot a saucer in the sky, but to also keep it in clear focus was a daunting task.

I suspect that today's sky-watchers are thrilled with modern camcorders, if for no other reason than the inclusion of *automatic focus control*. Thanks to millions of calculations processed while shooting, a camcorder can do an amazing job of keeping objects in focus. Sometimes, however, the camera performs its job too well.

Automatic focus versus manual focus

Digital camcorders use automatic focus by default. Although they include some sort of manual focus control (which is often a small dial that's hard to adjust in the middle of shooting), most likely it's not the type of focus ring found on your 35mm still camera. Nonetheless, don't be tempted to let automatic focus dominate your shots.

Auto focus tends to focus everything in view, causing footage to appear hyper-real at times (**Figure 2.9**). Your eyes don't bring everything into focus as you look around, so video that is predominantly focused can be distracting.

In an ironic twist, automatic focus can actually contribute to blurry images. The camera generally attempts to focus the objects in the foreground (which may appear on the periphery of the image and not be immediately visible to you), but that can throw off the focus in the rest of the shot and leave your subjects blurry (**Figure 2.10**).

If your camera is mostly stationary, experiment with manual focus to ensure that the objects you want to capture remain in focus.

Depth of Field

We usually want to keep things in focus, but when everything appears sharp, most scenes begin to look flat. Instead, highlight objects in the foreground by keeping them in focus, and separate them from the background by keeping it soft. When you increase this depth of field, you're more effectively simulating how a viewer's vision works, and subtly influencing what they should see. This works particularly well during interviews or scenes where a character is occupying the frame.

To increase depth of field:

1. Position the camera as far away from your subject as possible.

2. Use the camcorder's zooming controls to zoom in close to the subject.

3. Set the manual focus so that the subject is clear (**Figure 2.11**).

Figure 2.11 The background is out of focus and less vibrant compared to the foreground, which helps to visually separate the two.

Coverage

With some basics under your belt about framing your shots, we come to a bigger question: Which shots are needed to create a movie? If you're shooting a family event, you may think the question doesn't apply to you; after all, you shoot whatever happens, right?

Well, shooting the event itself is a good start, but you need more than that. And you need to make sure you have enough *coverage*, the footage that will give you plenty of room to work when you're editing in iMovie.

Shoot to edit

At the beginning of this chapter, I advised you to imagine the end result of your movie before you begin shooting. A similar notion is *shooting to edit*. In the days before anyone with a Mac could edit their movies, amateur filmmakers shot "in the camera," meaning they structured their shot process so that scenes fell sequentially in the order they would appear when the tape was played— "editing" was done in advance by planning what to shoot.

Now, you're shooting with the knowledge that your raw footage is going to be edited in iMovie. You don't have to shoot things in order, limit yourself to the main subject, or even use footage from the same session.

By way of example, suppose you're filming a family reunion. Immediately following the pick-up basketball game (where Uncle Barney surprised everyone with 32 points and a slam dunk), you shoot a few minutes of a wood-pecker perched on a nearby tree. Then you return to the festivities. The woodpecker has nothing to do with the family reunion, so you may not even use it in your final video—or perhaps you'll pop a few seconds of it into the beginning to show what a beautiful, nature-filled location everyone enjoyed.

COVERAGE

As another example, to round out your movie you want to show the sunset and then fade to black. Unfortunately, the sunset footage you shot wasn't as memorable as you remembered, so instead you grab 20 seconds of sunset footage you took on another location and insert that into your movie. Unless it's painfully obvious that the two locations are different (the presence of a sandy beach where before you were in the middle of a forest, for example), no one will know the difference, and your movie will end stronger. In each example, you had extra footage at your disposal because you were shooting to edit.

Types of coverage

When shooting a feature-length motion picture, a director will use multiple camera setups to shoot as much coverage as possible. So in one scene, the camera may shoot both actors in the frame, each actor from one or more different positions, and various combinations of points of view. The goal is to present a scene in the edited movie where the camera position is integral to the scene's mood or content.

◆ **Establishing shot.** This is usually an overview shot that's wide enough to let the viewer know the setting and which characters inhabit the scene (**Figure 2.12**). It can be a sign reading "Welcome to Twin Falls," a shot of someone's house, or a shot of a room. The important thing is that the establishing shot provides a physical geography of where objects appear. (This technique is used to great effect in dozens of movies and television shows: you see an establishing shot of the Chicago skyline and assume that the action takes place there, even though the actual filming took place in Vancouver.)

Figure 2.12 An establishing shot gives the viewer a sense of where the next scenes will occur, such as this shot of a campsite.

Figure 2.13 A medium shot is typically close enough to include two or three people.

Figure 2.14 A close-up focuses on one person or object that occupies most of the frame.

◆ **Medium shot.** Most shots end up as variations of medium shots. Generally, this shot is large enough to frame two or three people's torsos, although it can vary between a shot of a single person or half of a room (**Figure 2.13**).

◆ **Close-up.** The screen is filled with part of a person or object (**Figure 2.14**). Close-ups usually show a person's head and shoulders, but can also push in closer (known as an extreme close-up) so you see only the person's eyes. Other examples of close-ups include shots of a person's hands, or any object that occupies the entire frame.

◆ **Cut-away shots.** Sometimes referred to as B-roll footage, cut-aways are shots of associated objects or scenes that aren't necessarily part of the central action in a scene. An example would be the view from a ship traveling through a passage, which cuts away to a shot of the darkening sky, then returns to the ship safely emerging from the passage. The woodpecker footage mentioned in the family reunion example earlier could easily be used as a cut-away shot. Cut-aways often prove invaluable when you need to cover up a few frames of a glitch or when cutting and shortening interviews.

◆ **In points and out points.** If possible, give yourself some shots that can be used to enter or exit a scene, sometimes known as in points and out points. For example, if you're shooting an interview and your subject has just declared his intention to walk on Mars, don't immediately stop recording. Hold the camera on him as he finishes speaking, then perhaps pan down to his desk where a model of his rocket ship is mounted.

✔ Tips

- Linger on shots when you can. It's far easier to cut footage out than to add it back in later (especially if it's vacation footage or something similar...unless you *really* need to rationalize a trip back!).

- How long should you hold on to a shot? First of all, don't automatically shut off the camcorder just when the action has stopped. Stay for a few seconds or minutes to let the emotion of a scene dissipate. This is true when you're doing interviews or shooting wildlife. You can always trim it later in iMovie.

- Remember that a camcorder isn't like a still camera. I've seen people rotate the camcorder 90 degrees as they would a still camera in an effort to shoot a "taller" image (**Figure 2.15**). Unfortunately, no matter how you shoot, the end result will still be a horizontal image—it's not a print that you can view vertically.

  (That said, your footage *can* be salvaged. See Chapter 10 to learn how.)

- Here's a tip I came across while on a soggy camping trip. When shooting in poor weather, you'll need to protect your gear. You can buy hoods and covers and other accessories, which are fine but add bulk and can be pricey. Instead, I have a fleece vest that I use to cover the camera: the lens points through one arm hole, protecting it from the rain but still giving enough room for me to operate the camera. I wouldn't use it in a downpour, but it's come in handy several times when the weather has been sketchy.

Figure 2.15 Resist the temptation to rotate your camcorder as you would a still camera to take "vertical" shots, because in video they'll look like this.

THE CAMERA IN MOTION

3

My digital camcorder is small enough that I can take it almost anywhere. While we're driving to work, my wife will occasionally grab the camera out of my bag and start shooting anything that catches her eye: a brilliant sunrise, the way Seattle's skyline materializes on a foggy morning, rows of orange-tipped trees alongside the roadway in the fall. Although we initially bought the camera to take with us on vacation, it has turned into an unofficial chronicler of our lives.

One of the advantages of a small camera is that it easily moves with you. However, when you're shooting, motion can become a character in its own right. Slowly moving across a scene imparts a different feeling than quickly scanning your surroundings, for example. This chapter addresses the most common ways of moving the camera to add motion to your movie, including the number one rule: Don't move.

Don't Move

It's time to go watch TV again (hey, this moviemaking stuff is easy!). Turn to a scripted dramatic show and note how often the camera moves. I don't mean how often the *camera is moved*, which provides different angles of the same scene, but how often the camera is actually moving—not much. When it does move, such as when following a character through a set, the movement is smooth and measured.

As much as possible, limit your camera's movement. You want action that emotionally affects the viewer, which is more likely to happen when the camera is stationary and focused on the contents of a scene. A shot that's bouncing, zooming, or otherwise sloshing about like a drunk at happy hour is a scene where the movement is distracting from the action. Of course, there are times when motion is called for: can you imagine reality-television shows like *COPS* or *The Amazing Race* using stationary cameras? I imagine it's difficult enough to chase a suspected criminal down a dark alley and over a chain-link fence without asking him to pause for a few minutes while the crew sets up its lights and tripods.

Staying still has another practical benefit: excess movement causes blurring in your images (**Figure 3.1**). Our eyes do a good job of pulling detail out of motion blur, but there's a limit to how often they can tolerate fuzzy swabs of color streaking across the screen.

✔ Tip

- To move the camera and keep it steady, consider building your own Steadicam-like rig. You can find instructions in Dan Selakovich's book *Killer Camera Rigs that You Can Build* (www.dvcamerarigs.com).

Figure 3.1 Sudden camera moves introduce blurriness to your footage. Try to keep the camera stationary for most of your shots, if possible.

But If You Must Move...

Okay, you don't have to remain completely still when shooting. In fact, motion can be particularly effective—in moderation. A little motion can go a long way.

Case in point: film director Steven Soderberg. If you watch one of his movies, you'll notice that the camera is almost always in motion, but just barely. A scene in *Ocean's Eleven* stands out in my mind, where a group of main characters steals a device from a research university. In the shot, you're looking down the side of their getaway van toward a set of doors where the crooks will emerge with the device.

It would have been simple to lock the camera down in a fixed location and shoot the actors coming out of the doors. Instead, Soderberg *very slowly* pushes in on a dolly (see "Dollying," later in this chapter). The camera only moves perhaps one or two feet, but the subtle motion draws your attention to the door in a way that a motionless shot would not.

Figure 3.2 Optical zoom and automatic focus can be a great combination when you're shooting something from far away.

Start with the camera zoomed out...

...and slowly zoom in...

...then hold on the zoomed-in image before slowly zooming back out.

Figure 3.3 Quick zooms in and out are effective ways to instill headaches in your viewers. Instead, slowly zoom in, hold, then slowly zoom out. This technique gives you good, clear footage at several distances.

Zooming

Now that I've lectured on the evils of moving your camera, let's get into the realities of the types of motion you'll encounter. To start, let's look at one of the most common trouble-makers, the zoom control.

When you bought your camera, the first thing you probably did was play with the zoom control. It's usually a rocker switch that moves between W (wide) and T (telephoto), and enables you to view distant objects. Combined with a camera's automatic focus feature, especially when shooting in the field, zooming can get you closer to your subject (**Figure 3.2**).

However, the control can be sensitive, leading to abrupt or too-quick zooms in and out. A better approach is to smoothly zoom in on your subject, hold for a bit, then slowly zoom out (**Figure 3.3**). Practice with the control to get a feel for how much pressure is needed, and try to run through the shot a few times before you actually record it.

✔ Tips

- If you missed the memo in Chapter 1: Turn off the digital zoom feature of your camera. The camera tries to enlarge the pixels, thereby appearing to zoom beyond its optical limit. All you really end up with is large blocky pixels.

- Sometimes you want an abrupt zoom, either because it enhances the action or because you don't have time to shoot, stop recording, zoom in, then begin recording again. In the latter case, zoom quickly and hold onto the shot—you can edit out the actual zoom later in iMovie.

- A good zoom can be handy when you're not recording. If you're not toting a pair of binoculars, your camcorder will help you see objects in the distance.

Dollying

Dollying is similar to zooming, in that the camera moves in toward (or away from) a subject. However, a dolly shot doesn't use the zoom control at all. In feature film shoots, a dolly is a platform that holds the camera and rides on rails similar to railroad tracks. When filming, one or more people (known as grips) push the dolly, resulting in a smooth shot.

When you zoom, the camcorder's lens is simulating the appearance of moving closer to your subject. When dollying, you're moving the camera physically closer. The difference is especially pronounced in the background (**Figure 3.4**).

✔ Tips

- As with zooming, you want to ease in and out of a dolly shot. Grips aren't just people who push equipment around. A good grip can accelerate and decelerate smoothly and, often more importantly, *consistently* during multiple takes.

- A dolly shot is a professional-looking camera move, but it's likely you don't have a dolly setup or want to spend the money to rent one. Instead, choose from a number of alternative dollies. Wheelchairs are great (and comfortable for filming!), and skateboards also work in a pinch. It doesn't matter so much *how* you get the shot, only that the shot turns out the way you want it.

Zoomed in

Pushed in on dolly, no zoom

Figure 3.4 These two shots are similarly framed, but look at the orange building in the background to see how the two approaches differ.

Automatic

1/2000 shutter speed

Figure 3.5 Higher shutter speeds can make fast-moving objects appear clearer.

Changing Shutter Speed

Your camcorder doesn't have a shutter in the traditional sense. There's no little door that opens and closes quickly to control the amount of light that gets through the lens. However, camcorders can simulate shutter speed by controlling how quickly the CCD sensors refresh the image being recorded, which is measured in times per second. A normal shutter speed is approximately 1/60th of a second, meaning the CCD samples an image 60 times per second.

Why change shutter speed? Using a higher setting is good for capturing fast-moving action like sporting events. The blur caused by moving objects is substantially reduced at speeds of 1/4000 or 1/8000, creating frames that contain very little blurring (**Figure 3.5**). You'll need to experiment with your camera's settings, though; a high shutter speed can also make the image appear to strobe, or flash artificially.

✔ Tips

- Faster shutter speeds require more light. If you think of a traditional shutter, not as much light enters the camera when the shutter is closing more times per second. So a dimly lit room can appear even darker at a high shutter speed.

- Your camcorder is probably changing shutter speeds without your knowledge. On Auto setting, it detects what kind of light is present, and if it detects fluorescent lighting—which flickers imperceptibly to our eyes, but can cause havoc on a digital recording—the shutter speed automatically changes to compensate.

Panning

Film has the great advantage of width: its wider aspect ratio captures landscape images in a way your regular video camcorder can only dream about. (One of the advantages of shooting in HD is that it's always widescreen.) However, you can pivot the camera left or right to shoot that landscape and not disrupt the scene with too much motion. This side-to-side movement is called panning, and is a common tool in a director's box of shots. A similar shot, tilting, moves the camera up and down, though it's not used as frequently.

Figure 3.6 Frame your shots when panning so that subjects walk into the shot, not out the edges.

To pan a scene:

1. Mount your camera on a tripod for best results, or hold it as steady as you can.

2. Determine where the pan will begin and end.

3. Begin recording at the first point, and pivot the camera left or right at an even pace. If your camera is not on a tripod, swivel your body steadily at the hips.

4. When you reach the end point of your pan, stop recording.

Pan ahead of subjects

A panning shot often follows a subject from one side of the screen to the other, but think of your composition as you do this. Don't just center the subject in the frame. Instead, provide space into which the person can walk by panning ahead of him (**Figure 3.6**).

Figure 3.7 It's either you or the camera—the world just doesn't naturally tip like that.

✔ Tips

- To help stabilize the camera while you're holding it, pull your elbows in close to your body, hold the camera with both hands, and keep a wide stance.

- If you're using a tripod, be sure to get a fluid-head tripod. It's more expensive than your standard unit, but allows for much smoother motion.

- As it turns out, the biggest problem with panning isn't moving the camera smoothly. Your top concern should be: Is the horizon level? If the camera isn't exactly even with the horizon, panning will give the effect of moving uphill or downhill (**Figure 3.7**).

- Panning doesn't have to involve rotating the camera around a central axis. Use a dolly setup (see "Dollying," earlier) to move the camera from side to side.

4

LIGHTING

Unless you plan to shoot with the lens cap on, you'll have to come to grips with lighting in your videos. Put simply, you want to have enough light to see what's being filmed, but not so much that it blows out the camcorder's sensors with pure white. You also don't want scenes that are so dark you can't see what's going on.

When a Hollywood film crew shoots a movie, the lighting you see is enhanced (or outright artificial—even the most natural-looking sunlight coming through a window is likely a big spotlight on the other side of the wall). You don't need to go to those extremes, of course. Most often your lighting rigs will entail the sun, some lamps, and maybe a spotlight or two.

What's important is that you know how basic lighting works, and how to take advantage of it to ensure that the objects you're shooting don't turn out to be dark, talking blobs when you're editing.

Hard and Soft Light

There are infinite possible combinations of light, which can seem daunting when you're shooting video. Fortunately, for our purposes we can break light into two broad categories: hard and soft.

◆ **Hard light.** The term hard light refers to the light produced by a direct source, which creates shadows with clearly defined edges (**Figure 4.1**). Hard light tends to be bright, like the sun at midday.

◆ **Soft light.** In contrast, soft light isn't as direct, and produces shadows that are blurred at the edges or fade away (**Figure 4.2**). Soft light is typically light filtered by artificial means (such as hoods and filters attached to the light) or by natural means (such as clouds, fog, or shade).

In general, soft light is better to film by, because it gives you more levels of brightness and accentuates natural textures. Hard light creates a lot of contrast, limiting the brightness levels because you see either high-intensity light or deep, dark shadows.

✔ Tip

■ If lighting is particularly important to a scene, add a video monitor to your list of equipment to bring on a video shoot. Although your camcorder offers a viewfinder and an LCD, you won't know how the image will look on a TV screen until you see it projected on a monitor. The camera's LCD is great for viewing the content you're capturing, but LCDs can often display images brighter than they're being recorded; or, if you're outside, the LCD's pixels can get washed out by the sunlight.

Figure 4.1 Hard light creates sharp, clearly defined shadows. A bright halogen lamp is providing the light.

Figure 4.2 Soft light diffuses the shadows, making them blurry or even fade out gradually. In this case, a white t-shirt was put in front of the halogen bulb to dampen its intensity. (Hey, we're real high-tech at the Carlson world headquarters.)

White balance, indoors

White balance, outdoors

Figure 4.3 Many camcorders feature the capability to adjust the color temperature they display.

Color Temperature

White light is a combination of all the colors of the spectrum, as you've seen when playing with a prism or looking at a rainbow. As such, it's not going to always be white while you're filming—a myriad of factors can make images appear with a colored cast, leading to video footage that looks a little too green, or blue, or any number of shifts.

Your camcorder automatically adjusts to compensate for this *color temperature* of the light by setting the white balance. Essentially, this is the color that the camera sees as white, causing the camera to adjust the display of the rest of the colors based on this setting. You probably have a few basic controls for changing the setting, such as Auto, Indoor, or Outdoor presets (**Figure 4.3**).

You may also be able to specify the white point manually by selecting Manual and filming a sheet of white paper in the environment where you'll be shooting; the camera uses the values it captured as the basis for displaying the other colors.

Three-Point Lighting

If you have more control over the way your scene is lit, try to use a basic three-point lighting setup. This allows for plenty of light to illuminate the scene, while also reducing deep shadows. A three-point setup consists of a *key light*, a *fill light*, and a *back light* (**Figure 4.4**).

The key light is the primary light source in your scene, and usually the brightest. The fill light is softer, filling in the shadows and adding texture, and is often dimmer than the key light to avoid washing out the image and flattening it. The back light is often small, focused, and used to help separate the scene's subject from the background.

As an easy example, let's say you're setting up to shoot an interview (**Figure 4.5**). Remember, this is just a basic configuration—you can position the lights any way you choose.

To set up three-point lighting:

1. With the camera facing the interview subject, position the key light to the right and slightly forward of the camera. Raise the light so that it's at a 35- to 45-degree angle, pointing down at the subject.

2. Position the fill light to the left of the camera and subject, approximately halfway between the two. The fill prevents deep shadows caused by the key.

3. Place the back light behind the subject, raised a bit higher than the key light, and aimed so that it illuminates the back of the subject's head and shoulders.

Fill light   Back light   Key light

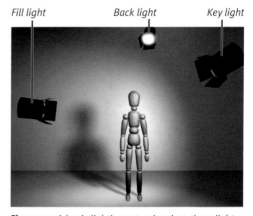

Figure 4.4 A basic lighting setup involves three lights, though of course you can use more (or less).

Key light only

Key light and fill light

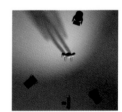

Key, fill, and back lights

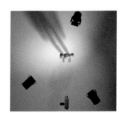

Figure 4.5 You could use just a key light, a fill and key, or any other combination of lights. Shown here is the progression of adding lights.

Figure 4.6 A strong light source behind your subjects can easily make them appear as silhouettes.

✔ Tips

■ Your camcorder is programmed to automatically adjust the exposure (the amount of light coming in). You've probably seen this happen when you move from a bright area to a dark one, as details come into view after a second or two. To minimize this extreme change of contrast, break up your shots so the camera can make the adjustment when you're not filming.

■ You've seen the silhouettes. When the key light is behind your subject—whether it's the sun, an especially bright white wall, or a lamp in the background—the camera picks up on the light area in favor of the dark, and pretty soon the person in your video looks like a mob informant protecting his identity (**Figure 4.6**). Try to shoot with the light coming from behind you or from one side, so the light falls on the person or object you're filming.

■ When a back light spills directly into the frame, you get the visual artifact known as lens flare. Repositioning your light usually fixes the problem.

■ Keep in mind that you don't need to raid a professional camera store and stock up on lighting equipment. You probably have all the lights you need at home or in your office, if you're willing to move things around a bit. Just be careful not to shed too much light onto a scene, which will make it appear flat and less interesting.

■ Three-point lighting is a good minimum starting point. On some productions, dozens of light sources may be used to light a scene properly.

Bounce Cards and Reflectors

You don't need a truckload of lights to illuminate your scene. A common and easy solution for shedding more light on your subject is to use a bounce card or reflector. These are either pieces of cardboard, cloth, or wood that are colored white, gray, or silver to reflect light into shadowy areas. You can buy inexpensive flexible reflectors that twist into a compact circle for storage. You could also create your own reflectors—white poster board covered with aluminum foil on one side, for example.

Have someone hold the reflector, or mount it on something, and aim its reflection as you would with a fill light.

✔ Tips

- Bounce light onto a person's face, but don't bounce it into their eyes. Yeah, it's a mean thing to do, but more importantly (for our purposes, anyway), it makes him squint, hiding the eyes, which are often a subject's most compelling feature.

- iMovie includes the capability to adjust brightness and contrast in a movie clip, but it won't fix a poorly lit scene. In fact, cranking up the brightness often washes out the image, because the setting is applied evenly throughout the frame. See Chapter 10 to learn how to apply video adjustments in iMovie.

Figure 4.7 Shooting in the middle of the day can create sharp shadows.

Shooting Outside

It's one thing to configure lighting in a dark room where you have absolute control. But the rules become much more slippery when you're filming outside, where the sun and clouds can change the lighting from moment to moment. No matter where you're filming, you can make choices that take advantage of the weather.

◆ Avoid shooting in the middle of the day when the sun is directly overhead. A key light from above casts shadows down across the face, which obscures a person's eyes and can give the appearance of a hung-over Frankenstein (**Figure 4.7**).

◆ Clouds are your friends. A good layer of cloud cover is an excellent diffuser of sunlight, providing a more even level of light in your scene. Coupled with a few well-placed bounce cards and a fill light, a typical cloudy day can provide warmer tones than you might expect.

◆ Shade is also your friend. Again, you want to minimize high-contrast key light-ing and enhance the balance between shadows and fill light. Move to the shade of a tree (which can also provide its own unique shadow textures, depending on the tree) or to the side of a building.

◆ To maximize natural light, shoot early or late in the day, when the sun is near the horizon. The light isn't as harsh, you can get some very intriguing shadows, and the color of the scene is generally warmer and more inviting.

✔ Tip

■ If you must shoot in the middle of a sunny day, put some light-colored fabric above your subject to act as a diffuser.

CAPTURING AUDIO

Video gets all the attention. When new camcorders are released, companies hype the image resolution, the color fidelity, the zoom ratios, optics...oh, and there's a microphone in there somewhere, too.

Well, you'll discover soon enough how important audio is. You can spend hours setting up your lighting and composition, but if the sound is poor, your scene is poor. The good news is, for most casual shooters, the built-in mic will capture what you're filming. Some cameras include controls for varying input levels, while most others offer automatic gain control (AGC) to manage the input without your involvement. However, even if you're going to be filming informally, consider purchasing a separate microphone.

As with lighting, you can spend your life learning the complexities of audio production. This chapter is intended as an overview of some options available for capturing audio.

Headphones

If sound is at all important to you, pack a pair of headphones when you go shooting (**Figure 5.1**). You can use almost any old pair (earbud-style headphones, for example, are extremely portable), but what's important is that you can hear what your camcorder is recording.

When you're standing behind the camera, your ears are naturally picking out the audio in the scene and ignoring other ambient noises. Your camera's microphone isn't nearly as sophisticated, and does its best to maintain a level input based on all the noise in the immediate vicinity. Camcorder mics can also be sensitive to movement, picking up the sound of you shifting the camera or adjusting the focus.

A pair of headphones screens out the noise around you and gives you a direct bead on what the camera is hearing. And, it's the best audio troubleshooting device on the market: if you can't hear your subject, you'll know right away, instead of later on when you're editing in iMovie.

Figure 5.1 Wearing headphones while shooting is the only accurate way to know what your camera is recording.

Built-in microphone

Figure 5.2 The camera's built-in microphone is good, but it's susceptible to picking up noise from the camera and doesn't record distant subjects too well.

Your Camcorder's Microphone

I don't want to give the impression that a camcorder's built-in microphone is a flimsy afterthought. On the contrary, it's a sophisticated device that does the best it can, given the circumstances. Where it falls flat at times is with its placement: Because camcorders are so small, there isn't much room for a microphone (**Figure 5.2**), so you're bound to pick up sounds that the camera is making (such as the motor advancing the tape, or the zoom control adjusting the lens).

Another limitation is distance. The most important factor when recording audio is the distance between the microphone and subject—the closer the better. If you're filming a birthday party, for example, you're likely to be right in the action and will pick up audio pretty well. But what about when you're doing an interview? You want the person's comments to be picked up clearly, but you don't want the camcorder to be in her face. If you're shooting from a moderate distance away (see "Depth of Field" in Chapter 2), the microphone won't pick up the sound clearly.

✔ Tip

- Camera manufacturers are starting to realize that audio recording can be a compelling selling point. A few camcorders record in Dolby 5.1 stereo surround sound.

Make a Movie in a Hurry

For this overview, we're going to import video from a digital camcorder, assemble a short movie from the footage, edit the video, add transitions, titles, and a soundtrack, and then upload it to YouTube.com for others to view. More information can be found in the chapters referenced in parentheses.

To import footage (*Chapter 8*):

1. Connect the camcorder to your Mac using FireWire or USB cables, depending on the camera.

2. Switch the camera to Play or VCR mode and launch iMovie. The import window should appear.

3. Set the mode switch at the left side of the window to Automatic and press the Import button.

4. In the dialog that appears, enter a name for the new Event where the video will be stored and then click OK (**Figure 6.1**). All footage on tape or memory (depending on model) is imported.

To assemble your movie (*Chapters 9 and 10*):

1. In the Event Browser at the bottom of the screen, move your mouse pointer over the video thumbnails to preview the footage; to play a clip in real time, double-click it or position the mouse pointer over a clip and press the spacebar.

2. Choose a clip that you want to add to your movie and click its thumbnail to select a four-second portion of a clip; drag the left or right edge to adjust the selection (**Figure 6.2**).

3. Click and hold in the middle of the selection and then drag it to the Project Browser (**Figure 6.3**). (You can also click

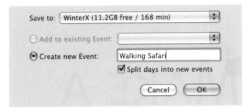

Figure 6.1 Every batch of imported video is saved as an Event in iMovie's Event Library.

Figure 6.2 Drag to select the video footage you want to include in your movie.

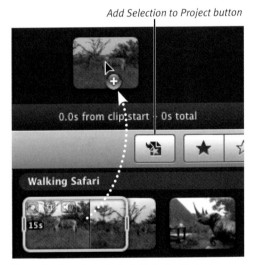

Figure 6.3 Drag the selected clip to the Project Browser to add it to your movie.

Figure 6.4 Congratulations, you've created a rough cut of your movie!

Figure 6.5 Click the Trim icon to edit a clip.

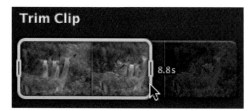

Figure 6.6 When you click the Trim icon, the Project Browser is replaced by the Trim Clip editor.

Photos button

Figure 6.7 iMovie can use photos from other Apple programs such as iPhoto and Aperture.

Figure 6.8 Drag a photo from the Photos Browser to your movie to create a picture with the Ken Burns Effect applied.

the Add Selection to Project button, or simply press the E key.) The clip is now part of your movie.

4. Continue adding clips to the Project Browser; in no time you'll have a rough cut of your movie (**Figure 6.4**). You can double-click in the browser, or position the mouse pointer on a clip and press the space bar, to play the video in the Viewer.

5. If you want to rearrange the order of the clips, select one and drag it to a new location. Dropping it onto an existing clip splits that clip at the point where you released the mouse button.

To edit clips (*Chapter 10*):

1. Trim the length of a clip by first clicking to select it and then clicking the Trim icon that appears (**Figure 6.5**).

2. In the Trim Clip editor that appears, drag the left or right edge of the clip to change its duration. Footage that appears within the yellow box will be visible in your movie. Other footage (dimmed) is hidden; you can always get it back later if needed (**Figure 6.6**). Click Done to return to the Project Browser.

3. Continue trimming clips until you're happy with the length of the movie.

To add a photo from iPhoto (*Chapter 11*):

1. Click the Photos button (or press Command-2) to view a list of photo sources on your computer (**Figure 6.7**).

2. Choose a photo below the Photos list and drag it to the Project Browser (**Figure 6.8**). Dragging an Event adds all images from that event. The Ken Burns Effect is applied by default, which you can edit later if you choose.

To add a transition (*Chapter 13*):

1. Click the Transitions button (or press Command-4) to display thumbnails of the available transitions (**Figure 6.9**).

2. Drag a thumbail from the Transitions Browser to the Project Browser; a solid green bar between clips indicates where the transition will appear when you release the mouse button (**Figure 6.10**).

To add a title (*Chapter 13*):

1. Click the Titles button to view the Titles Browser (**Figure 6.11**).

2. Drag a title thumbnail to the location in your movie where you want the title to appear (**Figure 6.12**).

   To make the title overlay the video, drag it directly on top of the clip (you can easily reposition it if you don't hit the precise location at first). Dragging a title to an empty space between clips creates the title on a black background.

   After releasing the mouse button, the title appears as a blue icon above the video.

3. With the title still selected, enter the title's text in the Viewer (**Figure 6.13**). Click Done to apply the title.

To add a soundtrack (*Chapter 12*):

1. Click the Music and Sound Effects button to view a list of audio sources that iMovie recognizes (**Figure 6.14**).

2. Preview a song by selecting it and clicking the Play button, or double-clicking the title.

3. When you've chosen one to use, drag it to the Project Browser and release it when the background turns green (**Figure 6.15**). This method sets the song as a background soundtrack; dropping the song onto a video clip adds the song

Transitions button

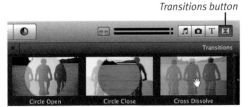

Figure 6.9 To preview each transition, hover the mouse pointer over the thumbnail.

Cross Dissolve transition

Figure 6.10 Drag a transition to the position between two clips. Each transition type has its own icon to easily tell what has been applied.

Titles button

Figure 6.11 Several titles in iMovie '08 incorporate motion effects.

Apply a title   *Title added*

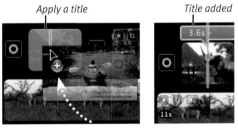

Figure 6.12 Drag a title thumbnail onto a clip to add it. The title appears as an icon above the video.

Figure 6.13 Type the title text directly into the Viewer.

Music and Sound Effects button

Figure 6.14 iMovie can access your iTunes and GarageBand libraries, but also includes sound effects.

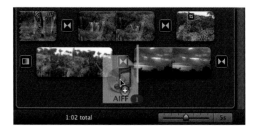

Figure 6.15 The green background tells you the song will be an underlying soundtrack.

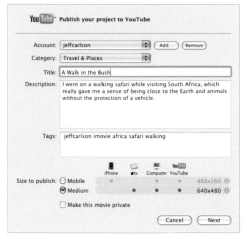

Figure 6.16 The capability to upload directly to YouTube enables many people to view the movie.

to that position in the movie (for simplicity, I'm sticking with a soundtrack in this example).

To share your movie to YouTube (*Chapter 15*):

1. When you're ready to make your movie public, choose YouTube from the Share menu. (YouTube isn't the only sharing method, of course, but it's one of the easiest for our example.)

2. In the YouTube dialog that appears, you may need to specify (or set up) your YouTube account. Click the Add button and follow the instructions; you'll need to do this only once.

3. Choose a category and enter a title, description, and any tags (which make it easier for people to find the movie) (**Figure 6.16**).

4. Choose a size for the final movie, Mobile or Medium, depending on how you expect people to watch the movie.

5. To share the movie only with people you choose, mark the checkbox labeled Make this movie private.

6. Click Next, read the YouTube Terms of Service, and then click Publish to encode and upload your movie to the Web.

7. After several minutes (depending on the movie's length and the published size), iMovie gives you the Web address and an option to send it to a friend.

✔ Tip

■ To watch the movie I created in this chapter, point your Web browser to http://youtube.com/watch?v=udMD8dQss3s

7

iMOVIE OVERVIEW

Getting iMovie '08

If you bought a Mac after August 2007, iMovie '08 should already be installed. Otherwise, you need to purchase iLife '08, Apple's $79 suite of digital hub applications (www.apple.com/ilife/), which includes iMovie, iDVD, iPhoto, iTunes, GarageBand, and iWeb.

If iMovie HD 6 is already installed, the iLife '08 installer does not overwrite it; earlier iLife installers would simply nuke the old version in favor of the new. Because iMovie '08 is a brand-new program, Apple knew that some people would want features from the old version that didn't transfer to the new.

If you purchased a Mac with iLife '08 pre-installed and you want to use iMovie HD 6, you can download it for free from www.apple.com/support/downloads/imovieHD6.html. The installer checks for the presence of iMovie '08, so this isn't a free way to upgrade to version 6 from something earlier.

iMovie runs only under Mac OS X 10.4.9 or later and only on a Mac containing an Intel processor, a Power Mac G5 (dual 2.0GHz or faster), or an iMac G5 (1.9GHz or faster).

Being a fan of the moviemaking process, I enjoy reading "behind the scenes" articles about how films are produced. In nearly all cases, the reporter interviews cast and crew at the movie set during shooting (and invariably makes it sound more exciting than it usually is). But filming is only one part of the production.

Rarely reported is the editing stage, when the editor (often with the director) spends long hours in a dark editing room—sometimes for many months—shaping hours of raw footage into what we eventually see in a theater. They grab the best takes from each day's shooting, assemble them according to the storyline, and then add transitions, audio, special effects, and whatever else is required for that particular flick.

The process of making your digital video is similar (minus the reporters and possibly the long hours). By this point you've shot your footage, but that doesn't mean you have a movie. Here's where iMovie and digital non-linear editing can take your mass of video and audio and turn it into a movie. This chapter introduces iMovie, making sure you have the tools you need to get started, and giving you an overview of the program's unexpectedly powerful yet simple interface.

Managing Projects

The first thing to do is launch iMovie. This step may seem absurdly obvious, but stick with me for a minute. Go to your Applications folder in the Finder and launch iMovie by double-clicking its icon. If this is the absolute first time you've launched iMovie '08, after the title screen, you'll see a dialog asking if you want to create iPhoto thumbnails (**Figure 7.1**). Click Now to process the thumbnails (it doesn't take long) or Later to procrastinate and put off the decision.

iMovie opens with an empty project to get started (**Figure 7.2**); double-click the name to give it a title other than My First Project.

Creating a new project

Unlike previous versions of the software, iMovie '08 stores all your projects in one place instead of asking you to open a new file for each project. When you create a new project, it appears in the Project list. And for easier organization, you can put projects into folders.

To create a new project:

1. Click the Add button at the bottom of the Project Library, or choose New Project from the File menu (or press Command-N) (**Figure 7.3**).

2. In the dialog that appears, choose an aspect ratio for the project (**Figure 7.4**). iMovie can accept several formats and sizes, so pick the size you want the final movie to be. The project's aspect ratio can be changed later if you want (see ahead).

3. Give your project a descriptive file name.

To organize projects into folders:

1. Choose New Folder from the File menu.

2. Name the folder in the dialog that appears.

3. Drag a project to the folder (**Figure 7.5**).

Figure 7.1 If this is the first time you've launched iMovie, you're asked to generate thumbnails for movies stored in your iPhoto library.

Figure 7.2 Double-click the first project title to give it a new name and claim it as your own.

Figure 7.3 Click the Add button to create a new project.

Figure 7.4 Choose an aspect ratio to avoid black bars appearing on the final video.

Figure 7.5 Folders let you group related projects together and reduce clutter.

MANAGING PROJECTS

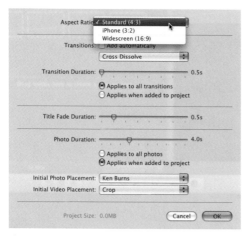

Figure 7.6 A project's aspect ratio can be changed at any time.

Figure 7.7 Work on a copy of a project by duplicating it, in this case via the contextual menu.

NTSC and PAL

iMovie's preferences let you choose the video standard: either NTSC - 30 fps or PAL - 25 fps. The setting applies only after you restart iMovie.

To change aspect ratio in a project:

1. In the Project list, select the project you want to change.

2. Choose Project Properties from the File menu, or press Command-J, to bring up the Project Properties dialog.

3. Choose a different option from the Aspect Ratio popup menu (**Figure 7.6**).

4. Click OK to apply the setting. iMovie automatically crops the footage to accommodate the new size (see Chapter 10 for more on cropping).

Duplicating and deleting projects

It's not uncommon to reach a fork in the editing road where you'd like to try a couple of different approachs. In that case, you can duplicate your project and work with a copy; if it doesn't work out as you hoped, simply go to the first version and delete the duplicate.

To duplicate a project:

1. Select a project in the Project list.

2. Choose Duplicate Project from the File menu. You can also right-click or Control-click the project's name and choose Duplicate Project from the contextual menu that appears (**Figure 7.7**). A new version with a number appended (such as "My First Movie 1") is created.

To delete a project:

1. Select a project in the Project list.

2. Choose Move Project to Trash from the File menu or the contextual menu, or press Command-Delete.

✔ Tip

- Duplicating a project does not duplicate the media files on your hard disk. By the same token, deleting a project does not erase the media files on disk.

iMovie's Interface

In iMovie, everything happens in one big window (**Figure 7.8**). Use the resize control in the lower-right corner to change the window's size, or click the green Zoom button in the upper-left corner to maximize the window.

The interface comprises three main areas: the Project Library, where you assemble your movie; the Viewer, where you preview clips; and the Event Library, where you store your footage. A toolbar bisects the window.

✔ Tips

- To help improve performance, try reducing iMovie's window to its minimum size. If the Monitor is smaller, iMovie doesn't need to expend as much processing power drawing video on the screen.

- The actual version number of the program is iMovie 7.1 (as of this writing), but Apple calls it either "iMovie" or "iMovie '08." I prefer the latter two, since this iMovie is actually version 1.0 (iMovie 6 was abandoned in favor of this new application). I'll refer to the version number only when needed.

Project List *Project Browser* *Viewer*

Event list *Event Browser* *Toolbar*

Figure 7.8 iMovie is broken down into three main sections: the Project Library (1); the Viewer (2); and the Event Library (3). The Project Library and Event Library each break down into a list and an area to browse the footage.

iMOVIE'S INTERFACE

Filmstrip   Clip (selected)   Playhead   Soundtrack

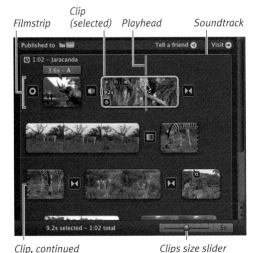

Clip, continued   Clips size slider

Figure 7.9 An edited movie in the Project Browser.

1/2s (half second)

2s (2 seconds)

All

Figure 7.10 Selecting a smaller time setting in the thumbnail control displays more images for each clip.

Make Some Breathing Room

To extend the width of the Project Browser and get a little larger workspace, click the Show/Hide Projects button.

The Project Library

The Project Library consists of the Project list, which is where you will find your iMovie projects, and the Project Browser, where you assemble and edit a movie.

Project Browser

The Project Browser displays your movie's clips from left to right and top to bottom, the same way you're reading this paragraph (**Figure 7.9**). The major components of the browser include (but are not limited to, as we'll see later):

◆ **Filmstrip.** All video clips appear in the filmstrip as a series of thumbnails. When a clip includes more thubnails than will fit on a line, iMovie indicates the visual break with a jagged edge. Transitions are indicated by icons between clips, and other elements such as titles and audio clips show up above or below the clips.

◆ **Playhead.** Move your mouse pointer to any point on the filmstrip and you'll see the playhead, a red vertical line that indicates which frame is currently showing in the Viewer.

◆ **Soundtrack.** A soundtrack is an audio file (usually a song) that plays behind the video. It's represented by a green field that literally sits behind the filmstrip. (See Chapter 12 for more on editing audio.)

◆ **Clips size slider.** This control determines how many thumbnails each clip displays. A setting of "5s" means iMovie is creating a new thumbnail for every 5 seconds of footage. Drag the slider to choose from "1/2s" (one frame for every half second, showing more images) to All (just one thumbnail for each clip) (**Figure 7.10**).

The Viewer

The Viewer is the window to your footage, displaying whatever frame of video appears at the current playhead location. It's also where you watch playback of your movie (**Figure 7.11**).

The Viewer can also be displayed in one of three preset configurations; for example, making the Viewer smaller frees up more room to browse the Event Library (**Figure 7.12**). From the Window menu, go to Viewer and then choose Small, Medium, or Large (or press Command-5, Command-6, or Command-7, respectively). Resizing the iMovie window as a whole (by dragging the lower-right corner) also changes the Viewer's size proportionally.

The Event Library

One new feature of iMovie '08 I particularly like is the Event Library, which allows me to find all of my footage in one place. As you'll see in the next chapter, iMovie organizes imported video into Events, which are listed in reverse chronological order in the Event list (**Figure 7.13**).

Clicking an Event displays its footage in the Event Browser. As with the Project Library, you can control how many thumbnails are visible by dragging the clips size slider located below the browser (**Figure 7.14**).

The Event list can also display more information than what originally appears.

To customize the Event list display:

◆ **Date ranges.** In iMovie's preferences, enable the option titled Show date ranges in Event lists to see the start and end dates of the footage (**Figure 7.15**).

Playhead

Figure 7.11 The Viewer displays the footage under the playhead and is where you watch movie playback.

Figure 7.12 With the Viewer set to Small, there's more work area for the Event Library (compare this to Figure 7.8 two pages back, which is set to Medium).

Figure 7.13 Video is organized by Event and listed in chronological order.

Clips size slider

Figure 7.14 The clips size slider controls how many images appear for the clips in the Event Browser.

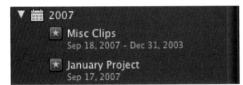

Figure 7.15 It can be helpful to see date ranges for Events to know at a glance when the video was shot.

Figure 7.16 Another way to view Events is by grouping them into months.

View Events by Volume button

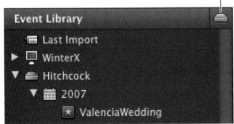

Figure 7.17 iMovie typically stores video on your Mac's internal hard disk, but it can also see other drives.

◆ **Events by month.** To break down the timeline further, choose Events by Month from the View menu (**Figure 7.16**).

◆ **Events by day.** Need more granularity? Choose Separate Days in Events from the View menu to have each day's footage broken out into separate rows in the Event Browser.

◆ **Volumes.** iMovie recognizes video stored on other hard drives. Click the View Events by Volume button, or choose Events by Volume from the View menu (**Figure 7.17**).

✔ Tips

■ Events that span two or more months are grouped under the month of the most recent video when the Events by Month option is enabled.

■ Even if you don't have the date ranges option enabled in iMovie's preferences, clicking an Event displays the range at the top of the Event Browser.

■ Click and drag the toolbar up or down to resize the main areas.

■ If a volume isn't currently connected, it won't show up in the Event Library when View Events by Volume is enabled. But when it comes back online, iMovie will include it in the list.

iMOVIE'S INTERFACE

Other view options

A few other features enable you to further customize the workspace for your editing convenience:

◆ **Swap the Event and Project libraries.** When the time comes to edit your project, you can gain some more working room by moving the Project Library to the area below the toolbar. (This arrangement is also similar to the position of the timeline in earlier versions of iMovie if you prefer that placement.) Click the Swap Events and Projects button, or choose Swap Events and Projects from the Window menu (**Figure 7.18**).

◆ **Change thumbnail size.** Drag the thumbnail size slider to enlarge or reduce the size of the filmstrips in both the Library browser and the Event Browser (**Figure 7.19**).

◆ **Use large font.** Maybe you have such a large, high-resolution display that everything looks small—or maybe your eyes just don't see as well anymore. In either case, you can enlarge the project and event titles by opening iMovie's preferences and choosing Use large font for project and Event lists (**Figure 7.20**).

✔ Tip

■ Hold the Shift key when clicking the Swap Events and Projects button to watch the swapping transition move in slow motion.

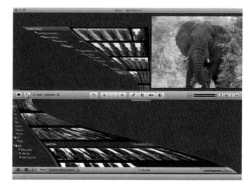

Figure 7.18 When you swap the Event and Project libraries, they shift places using the same stretchy effect used when minimizing items to the Dock.

Thumbnail size slider   *Filmstrip at largest size*

Figure 7.19 The thumbnail size slider controls the appearance of the filmstrips in both browsers.

Figure 7.20 The optional larger font size for the Project and Event lists is easier to read.

IMPORTING FOOTAGE

Whatever the source of your video—DV or HDV camcorder, digital still camera with a video recording feature, DVD, an iSight camera, or just movie files on your hard drive—it's easy to bring the footage you shot into iMovie for editing.

iMovie '08 now organizes everything in Events, which means you no longer need to remember where your iMovie projects are located. All your footage appears in iMovie's Event Browser for use with any project.

Importing Clips

Getting video footage into iMovie is a snap: connect your digital camcorder to your Mac via FireWire or USB, and start importing. Your only practical limitation is space on your hard drive—make sure you have plenty.

To connect via FireWire or USB:

1. Quit iMovie if it's running.

2. Plug the FireWire or USB cable into the Mac and the camcorder.

3. Switch the camcorder to VCR, Play, or PC mode (see the device's documentation).

4. Launch iMovie, which recognizes the attached camera and opens the Import window (**Figure 8.1**).

    If the Import window doesn't appear, click the Camera Import Window button (**Figure 8.2**) or press Command-I.

Importing from a DV camcorder

When you connect a tape-based camcorder, iMovie controls playback and import.

To import all footage from a tape:

1. In the Import window, set the mode switch to Automatic (**Figure 8.3**).

2. Click the Import button.

3. In the dialog that appears (**Figure 8.4**), specify the following:

    ▲ Choose a destination from the Save to popup menu. This is likely your computer's internal hard disk, but you can specify any hard disk that's mounted on the Desktop.

    ▲ If the footage is related to an existing Event you've already created, click the radio button marked Add to existing Event and choose the Event from the popup menu.

Figure 8.1 Launching iMovie with a camcorder connected automatically opens the Import window.

Figure 8.2 This button opens the Import window.

Figure 8.3 The Automatic mode imports a tape's worth of video without much work on your part.

Figure 8.4 Whenever you import footage, you need to create a new event or assign it to an existing event.

Figure 8.5 Imported footage appears in the Event Library and the Event Browser.

Rewind *Fast-Forward* *Stop* *Play*

Figure 8.6 Use the playback controls to locate the footage you want to import.

Figure 8.7 Click and hold the Rewind or Fast-Forward button while playing to review video at high speed.

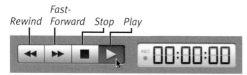

Figure 8.8 Choose a video source.

What Happened to Magic iMovie?

The Magic iMovie feature found in previous versions of iMovie is gone in iMovie '08, but some of its capabilities remain. The Automatic import mode will rewind your tape and bring in all clips. You can also automatically add a transition between each clip in the Project Properties dialog (see Chapter 13).

▲ Alternately, choose Create new Event and type a name in the field provided (or use the default iMovie gives you).

▲ If the footage spans multiple days and you want to organize them separately in the Event Browser, enable Split days into new events. Otherwise, deselect the checkbox.

4. Click OK. iMovie rewinds the tape, imports all of the footage, and then rewinds the tape again when it's done importing.

5. Click Done to exit the Import window. The Event and its footage appear in the Event Library (**Figure 8.5**).

To import clips from a tape:

1. Use the Import window's Playback controls to rewind or forward the camcorder's tape to the spot where you want to begin (**Figure 8.6**).

To review the video at high speed, click and hold the Rewind or Fast-Forward button (**Figure 8.7**).

2. Click the Import button and specify an Event (see Step 3 on the previous page).

3. Click the Stop button to stop importing.

4. Click Done to exit the Import window.

✔ Tips

■ iMovie supports having more than one video source attached to your Mac. Click the Camera button and select a camcorder from the popup menu (**Figure 8.8**).

■ Pressing the Esc key also closes the Import window.

■ Audio does not play back during import.

■ When you click the Import button, iMovie calculates how much video can be saved to your hard drive and displays the amount in the Save to popup menu.

IMPORTING CLIPS

71

Importing HDV footage

Importing high-definition video works the same as importing DV, with a couple of differences. iMovie transcodes the HDV footage into AIC (Apple Intermediate Codec) for editing, so importing does not happen in real time on many machines. This causes a lag between what you see on the camera's screen and in iMovie—the incoming video is stored in a buffer and then transcoded. The import speed is indicated below iMovie's Monitor (**Figure 8.9**).

For this reason, if you're capturing specific clips (versus an entire tape) don't use iMovie's playback controls to stop importing unless you're capturing in real time—you won't get the footage you expect. Instead, use the camera's LCD screen as a guide and press the camera's Stop button when you reach the end of the footage you want to capture. iMovie then transcodes the rest of the footage in its buffer.

If you're importing 1080i footage, iMovie offers a choice of size to import: Large or Full (**Figure 8.10**). The Large size makes it easier for iMovie to edit the footage on less-capable machines due to the processing power required to edit full-size HD.

✔ Tips

- HDV camcorders can also record DV footage, so make sure the camera is set to the corresponding format before you import.

- Although you can certainly go through your tape and import just the scenes you want, it's probably faster to import the whole thing and then delete what you won't use in iMovie; see Chapter 9.

- If you want to import your video to an external FireWire hard drive, get one with a speed of at least 7,200 RPM.

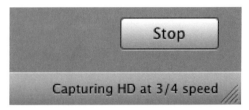

Figure 8.9 iMovie indicates the speed at which the video is being captured.

Figure 8.10 iMovie prefers to scale down 1080i video, but you can choose to import it at full size, too.

Large versus Full HD Video

The difference between the Large (960 x 540) and Full (1920 x 1080) sizes for HD video lies as much in iMovie's philosophy of editing as it does with image size. iMovie '08 assumes that you're not aiming for the absolute best possible image quality; that instead, you want to edit your home movies quickly and easily. Scaling HD video to half its resolution enables iMovie to work more efficiently.

Even if you choose Full, however, you may not gain an image quality advantage. iMovie appears to work internally at 960 x 540, so the video is still being reduced in size.

Most people will probably not notice a difference. If you're concerned about getting the best HD you can, it's worth using iMovie HD 6 or Final Cut Express.

Figure 8.11 In Manual mode, choose which clips to import from the camcorder.

Figure 8.12 Click the Play button to review a clip before importing it.

Importing from a tapeless camcorder

Cameras that record video on internal hard drives or memory cards aren't limited to the linearity of tape. The clips are stored wherever there's room on the media like any file on your computer. For that reason, iMovie takes a different importing approach.

To import from a tapeless camcorder:

1. In the Import window, set Automatic or Manual mode. Automatic imports all clips; Manual lets you choose which clips to bring into iMovie.

2. If you chose Automatic, skip to Step 3. If Manual, choose the clips you want to import by marking their checkboxes (**Figure 8.11**). By default, all clips are selected, so you may find it easier to click the Uncheck All button and then choose individual clips.

   To preview a clip, click to select it and press the Play button (**Figure 8.12**).

3. Click the Import All or Import Checked button (depending on the mode).

4. In the Event dialog, create a new Event or specify an existing one (see Step 3 under "Importing from a DV camcorder" earlier in this chapter).

5. For high-definition AVCHD video, choose a size for the imported footage.

6. Click Done to exit the Import window. iMovie imports the footage and transcodes it to AIC for editing.

✔ Tip

- When you're finished importing, be sure to eject the camcorder's media, which shows up as a mounted volume on your Desktop. Click the Eject button that appears beside the Camera popup menu.

To import live video from a DV camera:

1. Connect the camera to your Mac, and ensure that it has no tape inserted. If you're using Apple's iSight camera (built into many models), you can skip Step 3.

2. Launch iMovie.

3. Switch the camcorder to Camera or Record mode.

4. Bring up the Import window if it doesn't appear automatically (**Figure 8.13**).

5. Click the Import button; you don't need to use the camera's Record button. For an iSight, the button is labeled Capture.

6. In the Event dialog, choose an existing Event or create a new one. iMovie begins recording.

7. Click the Stop button to end recording.

8. Click Done to exit the Import window.

Figure 8.13 Capture live video (like this gem) using an iSight camera or a camcorder set to Record mode.

Importing Movies from iPhoto

Movies you shoot using a digital still camera can be imported into iPhoto, making it the best route to bring such videos into iMovie.

To import movies from iPhoto:

1. In the Event List, select iPhoto Videos (**Figure 8.14**).

2. Locate a video clip in the list.

3. Drag the file to the Project Browser (see Chapter 10).

Figure 8.14 iMovie recognizes movie files in your iPhoto library.

✔ Tip

■ When you mount a memory card, don't be surprised if iPhoto automatically launches: the Mac thinks you're importing photos. To change this behavior, open iPhoto, go to its preferences, and change the option labeled "Connecting camera opens" to No application.

The Biggest Hard Drive Isn't Large Enough

When you begin working with digital video, your concept of disk space changes forever. For example, one second of DV footage equals 3.6 MB on disk, which translates roughly to 13 GB of space per hour of video. One hour of high-definition footage occupies anywhere between 38 GB to 50 GB of space.

Fortunately, hard drives are cheaper every day: a quick search for a 500 GB internal drive turns up prices between $100 and $120 as of this writing (try www.dealmac.com). (To compare, that amount of money bought a 60 GB drive just a few years ago.)

RAID Storage

Most likely, buying one or two external hard drives will provide the storage you need. However, if you find yourself doing a lot of iMovie editing, consider buying or assembling a RAID (redundant array of inexpensive disks). By making two or more hard drives work in tandem, you can view their combined storage capacity as one volume, and potentially speed up performance.

A hardware RAID system, such as Apple's Xserve RAID, includes the hard drives in some type of enclosure, and handles all the data exchange among the drives by itself. (But at $6,000 and up, an Xserve is overkill for your iMovie needs. Companies are now offering drives of 1 terabyte (TB) or more by including multiple hard disks in a RAID configuration.) You can also connect a few drives via FireWire and configure them as a RAID using Apple's Disk Utility, or the $130 SoftRAID (www.softraid.com).

Importing video from old iMovie projects

iMovie '08 can import projects created in old versions of iMovie, but the result isn't what you may be hoping for. Basically, you'll get the raw footage with some basic editing applied (which is why you should finish any old projects in iMovie HD).

To import video from old iMovie projects:

1. From the File menu, choose Import iMovie HD Project.

2. Locate an iMovie HD project; if it's a 1080i project, choose whether to import the footage as Large or Full.

3. Click Import. The video is imported to the Event Browser, and the contents of the Timeline appear in the Project Browser; any transitions are converted to Cross Dissolve transitions.

✔ Tip

- If you're importing an MPEG video and it has no sound, convert it using the free MPEG Streamclip (www.squared5.com).

Importing Other Movies

iMovie is built on QuickTime, Apple's technology for playing and creating all sorts of digital audio and video, so you can import movie files into your projects.

To import a movie file into iMovie:

◆ Drag a QuickTime-compatible movie file from the Finder to an Event name in the Event Browser (**Figure 8.15**). Note that this action *moves* the file from its original location to the iMovie Events folder where the program stores its clips (see Chapter 9 for more information). If you'd rather *copy* the file, hold the Option key as you drag.

Or

1. In iMovie, choose Import Movies from the File menu.

2. Locate the file in the dialog and choose an Event (or create a new Event).

3. At the bottom of the dialog, choose whether to copy or move the original movie file to iMovie's preferred location (**Figure 8.16**).

4. Click the Import button. The clip appears in the Event you specified.

✔ Tips

■ The iMovie help files state that only QuickTime (.mov), MPEG-4, and DV formatted files can be imported, but other formats that QuickTime supports appear to import fine.

■ Most movie files are small in size and compressed, which is great for viewing on the Web but not so good-looking compared to a DV clip taken from a video camcorder (**Figure 8.17**).

Figure 8.15 Add a QuickTime-compatible movie to your project by dragging it to the Event List.

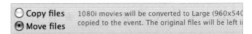

Figure 8.16 If you import movies using the dialog, be sure to choose whether the files are copied or moved.

Figure 8.17 To compare image resolution, I exported some DV footage (top) as a QuickTime file, then imported the file back into iMovie (bottom).

Figure 8.18 The quality of VHS tapes deteriorates dramatically, as evidenced by this 10-year-old frame. (The damage is more dramatic full-size; see it at www.jeffcarlson.com/imovievqs/vhs.html.)

Importing Footage from an Analog Camcorder

The process of importing footage from an analog camcorder in iMovie is much the same as when importing from a digital camcorder. However, you need a go-between device that converts the camcorder's analog signal to digital information on the Mac. Products from companies such as Canopus (www.canopus.com) or ADS Technologies (www.adstech.com) feature a FireWire port for connecting to your computer and RCA-style inputs for connecting to your camera; some devices also include an S-Video port.

To import from a non-DV camcorder:

1. Connect the conversion device to the Mac via FireWire, and to the camera using RCA or S-Video cabling.

2. Switch the camcorder to VCR or Play mode.

3. Bring up the Import window in iMovie, choose or create an Event, and click the Import button.

4. Push the camcorder's Play button.

5. When finished, click the Stop button to finish capturing video, and press the Stop button on the camcorder.

✔ Tip

■ Since you're importing converted analog data, iMovie doesn't automatically split clips according to scenes. You'll have to use iMovie's editing tools to trim and organize the clips, or manually start and stop importing according to scenes.

Importing Old VHS Tapes Using a DV Camcorder

If you own a digital camcorder, but still have some older VHS (or other format) tapes, you can bring that footage into iMovie to edit or even just to store digitally. Connect your VCR to your camcorder and record the contents of the VHS tape to the DV tape. Then you can import your footage into iMovie normally. (Or, use an analog-to-digital converter between the VCR and your Mac.)

Another option is to use a recent Sony DV camcorder, which performs an in-camera analog-to-digital conversion.

Analog tape doesn't last forever—save your wedding/graduation/school play on disk. As a gift to my wife on our tenth wedding anniversary, I digitized the video from the ceremony (shot by my uncle on VHS), cut together the highlights, and burned it to a DVD. I'm glad I did—the image and sound quality had severely deteriorated (**Figure 8.18**).

Extracting Footage from a DVD

So you burned a movie to DVD last year and want to snag some of that footage without trying to find the original MiniDV tape. Cinematize (www.miraizon.com), and DropDV (www.dropdv.com) can each extract the MPEG-2 video files stored on DVD discs. You can then import the footage into iMovie. DropDV is the more straightforward option, so I'll use that as the example program here.

To extract video from a DVD:

1. Insert a DVD disc into your Mac. If the DVD Player application launches, quit it.

2. Open the DVD's volume on the Desktop and locate the folder called VIDEO_TS.

3. Open the VIDEO_TS folder and locate the MPEG video files, which end in the suffix .VOB (**Figure 8.19**).

4. Drag the .VOB file onto DropDV. Depending on the movie's length, the conversion process could take a while (**Figure 8.20**).

5. Drag the .DV file that was created to your iMovie project to add it.

✔ Tips

■ Keep in mind that video you pull from a DVD is compressed, and will therefore be of lower quality than the original. But sometimes that's better than not having any footage at all.

■ If you're importing an MPEG video and it has no sound, convert it using the free MPEG Streamclip (www.squared5.com).

■ Be good, use copyrighted video footage legally, and only extract video from discs you own or have the rights to use. You know the drill.

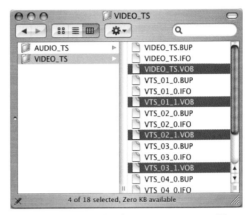

Figure 8.19 Video and audio on a DVD are stored in the VIDEO_TS folder as .VOB files.

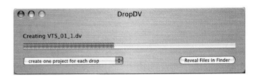

Figure 8.20 DropDV converts MPEG-2 formatted video files to DV files in a minimal interface.

Copy-protected DVDs

Some DVD extraction utilities won't work with commercial DVDs that have copy protection applied, but there's a workaround. Download the free utility HandBrake (handbrake.m0k.org) to pull even "secure" footage off most discs.

Obviously, I'm not advocating movie piracy here. But there are legitimate occasions when you might want to use a section of a movie (in a multimedia school report, for example), or copy a movie that you own to your laptop's hard drive to watch later without toting along a sleeve of discs when you travel.

MANAGING VIDEO

9

Now that you've imported all that video, what are you going to do with it? Make a movie, of course, and it's likely you've already done so (if you followed the steps in Chapter 6).

But what if your movie is more complex than a short uploaded to YouTube? What if you're faced with hours and hours of footage that needs to be culled and sorted before you can even begin to think about building the good clips into a movie? What if you want to find clips from an old project?

iMovie '08 includes powerful features for viewing, classifying, and keeping track of your footage—including several advanced capabilities that are initially hidden.

Skimming Video

One problem shared by many video editors is that you really need two storage locations for your video: one copy on disk and one copy in your head so you can recall what an entire clip holds, instead of just the first frame. One method iMovie uses to expose that footage is by displaying the filmstrip as a series of thumbnail images (see Chapter 8). Another is skimming.

To skim a clip:

1. Position the mouse pointer over a clip (in either the Project or Event Browser). The vertical red playhead indicates the current frame, which is displayed in the Viewer (**Figure 9.1**).

2. Drag the pointer left or right across the clip. As you drag, the playhead moves and the Viewer previews that section of the clip (**Figure 9.2**).

   The benefit to this approach is that you can drag at whatever speed you like—you don't have to view the footage in real time, or use VCR-style controls to rewind or fast-forward through the video.

Audio skimming

As you move the playhead, the audio plays at whatever speed you're moving the mouse pointer. Sometimes that's helpful to gauge overall volume, but typically I find it initially distracting.

To enable or disable audio skimming:

◆ Click the Audio Skimming button, choose Audio Skimming from the View menu, or press Command-K (**Figure 9.3**). The audio level indicators continue to display the volume levels but you won't hear the sound. (The sound is audible when playing clips normally.)

Playhead

Figure 9.1 When you skim a clip (bottom), the frame under the playhead appears in the Viewer (top).

Figure 9.2 This is the same clip as above, but skimming allows us to view the frames later in the clip (in this case, a pan across the landscape).

Audio Skimming button

Figure 9.3 Click the Audio Skimming button to toggle audio playback while skimming.

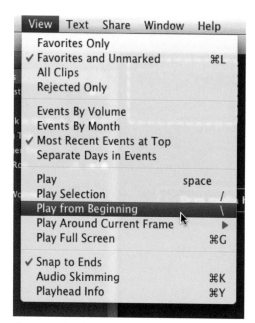

Figure 9.4 The View menu offers more playback options beyond just simply playing the movie.

Play button (Project Library)

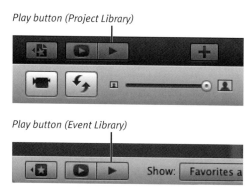

Play button (Event Library)

Figure 9.5 The Play buttons located below the Project Library and Event Library play video from the beginning of either section's filmstrip.

Playing Video

When I talk about "playing," I'm referring to watching video in real time. Naturally, you can play a clip or movie from start to finish. iMovie also provides a few approaches to watching selected clips or just a few frames near the playhead—good for when you're fine-tuning an edit or transition. And, of course, you can view your video in fullscreen mode for that almost-cinematic experience. (If you sit real close to the monitor, it's just like being in a theater...a very tiny, empty theater, but with less expensive popcorn!)

To play video:

◆ Position the playhead in a clip and press the spacebar. The video appears in the Viewer.

◆ Double-click a clip; the video begins playing from the position you clicked.

◆ To play a filmstrip from its beginning, no matter where the playhead is located, press the \ (backslash) key or choose Play from Beginning from the View menu (**Figure 9.4**).

You can also click the Play button in either the Project Library or the Event Library, depending on which footage you want to play (**Figure 9.5**).

To play selected video:

1. Click and drag to select a range of frames.

2. Press either the spacebar or the / (forward-slash) key, or choose Play Selection from the View menu. Playback stops at the end of the selection.

To play around the current frame:

1. Position the playhead in a clip.

2. Do one of the following:
   ▲ Press the [(left bracket) key to play 1 second around the playhead. iMovie starts playing from half a second before the playhead to half a second after the playhead (**Figure 9.6**).
   ▲ Press the] (right bracket) to play 3 seconds around the playhead (1.5 seconds on either side).

To play video full-screen:

1. Position the playhead in the filmstrip you want to watch.

2. Press Command-G, choose Play Full Screen from the View menu, or press the Play Full Screen button located next to the Play button in either the Project Library or Event Library. iMovie fills the screen with your movie.

   In fullscreen mode, you can also move the mouse pointer to reveal a filmstrip (**Figure 9.7**). This enables you to:
   ▲ Press the Play/Pause button to stop playback, or click on the filmstrip.
   ▲ When paused, drag to skim to any section of the video.
   ▲ Press the right or left arrow keys to move the playhead one frame at a time.

3. Press the Esc key to exit fullscreen mode.

✔ Tips

■ If you want fullscreen mode to remain active at the end of the movie, open iMovie's preferences and disable Exit fullscreen mode after playback is finished.

■ Also in preferences, choose an option from the Fullscreen playback size popup menu to control the movie's resolution (**Figure 9.8**).

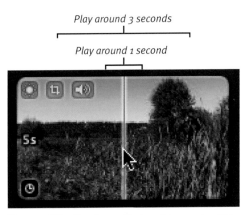

Figure 9.6 The Play Around feature lets you view the current frame in context without making you move the playhead manually. (This is a 5 second clip.)

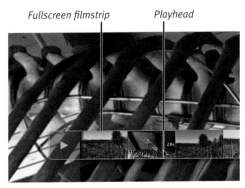

Figure 9.7 You can bring up a filmstrip and browse the movie without exiting fullscreen mode.

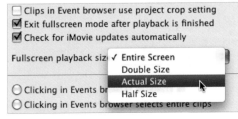

Figure 9.8 Choosing Actual Size from the popup menu offers a better reproduction of the movie's quality than Entire Screen, especially if you're working on a large display. However, you might not notice much difference if the video is high definition.

PLAYING VIDEO

Handle   Selection border   Duration of selection

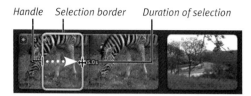

Figure 9.9 Click and drag to select a range of video.

Figure 9.10 Dragging a handle expands (or contracts) the selection.

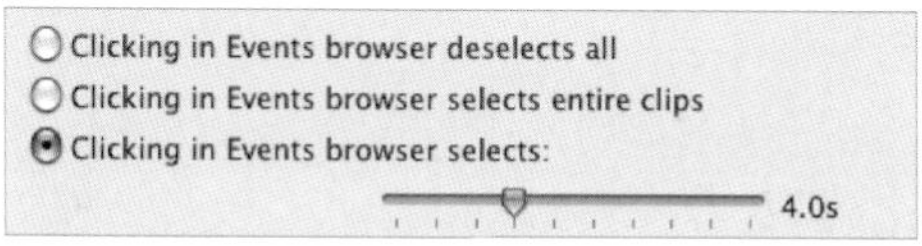

○ Clicking in Events browser deselects all
○ Clicking in Events browser selects entire clips
◉ Clicking in Events browser selects:
                                    4.0s

Figure 9.11 These options dictate what happens when you single-click a clip in the Event Browser.

Selecting Video

It's good to keep in mind that the filmstrip in iMovie is like a paragraph of text in a word processor. Just as you would highlight characters and words in text, you can select individual frames or full clips.

To select a portion of a clip:

◆ Click once on a clip. In the Event Browser, this automatically selects a four-second range of frames. (The duration can be changed; see below.) In the Project Browser, the entire clip is selected.

◆ Click and drag to select a custom range of frames, using the Viewer (which always shows the frame under the playhead) as a guide. The number to the right indicates the length of the selection (**Figure 9.9**).

To adjust a selection:

◆ Click and drag the handles on the edges of the selection box (**Figure 9.10**).

To change the default duration of a selection:

1. Open the preferences window by choosing Preferences from the iMovie menu, or by pressing Command-, (comma).

2. Choose one of the following options (**Figure 9.11**):

   ▲ **Clicking in Events browser deselects all** is helpful if you primarily drag to select frame ranges and don't want iMovie to select for you.

   ▲ **Clicking in Events browser selects entire clips.** This is self-explanatory; you can still select ranges by clicking and dragging.

   ▲ **Clicking in Events browser selects:** Drag the slider to set a default length of time for the selection.

To select an entire clip:

◆ With part of a clip selected, choose Select Entire Clip from the Edit menu, or press Command-A.

To select multiple clips:

1. Select a single clip or a portion of a clip.

2. Hold Shift and click another clip to include all the clips in between. Or, hold Command and click non-contiguous clips (**Figure 9.12**).

To deselect all clips:

◆ Choose Select None from the Edit menu, or press Command-Shift-A.

◆ Click an empty area in the browser (such as between clips).

Slipping (recentering) video

Slipping (which iMovie calls "recentering") is an editing technique that's particularly useful when you're working with fixed time periods. For example, suppose you select five seconds of footage at the beginning of a clip, but then realize that five seconds toward the clip's end would work better. Instead of separately adjusting the beginning and ending of your selection, simply recenter the clip.

To slip (recenter) a clip:

1. Make a selection.

2. Position the mouse pointer over the top or bottom of the yellow selection border. The cursor becomes a hand with an arrow in it (**Figure 9.13**).

3. Drag left or right to choose a new selection range without changing the selection's duration (**Figure 9.14**).

Figure 9.12 Command-clicking selected these non-contiguous clips. If I had Shift-clicked, all the clips would be selected.

Recenter cursor ———

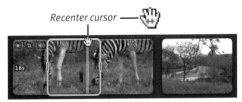

Figure 9.13 You know the cursor is positioned correctly to recenter the selection when you see a double-arrow icon appear within the hand.

Figure 9.14 After slipping the selection, the duration remains the same but different frames are included.

✔ Tip

■ With a selection made, you can expand or contract it by holding Shift and clicking a new frame of that clip instead of dragging the selection handles.

Figure 9.15 Select two or more Events to merge them into one Event.

Figure 9.16 Provide a new Event name, since you're essentially creating one from scratch.

Figure 9.17 The sparse amount of Day 1 footage is now merged with the plentiful Day 2 video.

Figure 9.18 Select a clip that will be the first video in the new Event you create.

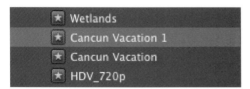

Figure 9.19 The clips following the split point now appear in their own Event, which iMovie labels with an incremental number.

Managing Events

When you import footage, iMovie's default behavior is to split each day's video into a separate Event (an option you can turn off during import; see Chapter 8). For more organizational control, you can merge or split Events.

For example, I have video from a recent trip where not much footage was shot on day one, but plenty was shot on the second day. I'd prefer to group them together as one Event.

To merge Events:

1. In the Event list, select the Events you wish to merge: Shift-click to select all Events between the ones you click, or Command-click to select discrete clips (**Figure 9.15**).

2. Choose Merge Events from the File menu, or Control-click and choose Merge Events from the contextual menu.

3. In the dialog that appears, type a name for the merged Event (**Figure 9.16**).

4. Click OK. The Events are merged into a single unit (**Figure 9.17**).

Similarly, you can split an Event to break out any content. In this example, I want a new Event for a boat trip from the second day.

To split an Event:

◆ In the Event Browser, select a clip (or portion of a clip) and choose Split Event Before Selected Clip from the File menu or Split Event Before Clip from the contextual menu (**Figure 9.18**). All clips from that point to the end of the Event are moved into their own Event (**Figure 9.19**).

✔ Tip

■ You can split an Event using the contextual menu based on the position of the playhead without selecting a clip.

Marking Footage

You're bound to end up with footage that never ends up in a movie, so why trip over it every time you go to the Event Browser? By the same token, you can easily identify which clips are better than others. It's easy to mark footage as a favorite or reject it (without deleting it, just in case).

To mark video as favorite:

1. In the Event Browser, select a range of video you like; it can be an entire clip, multiple clips, or a range of footage.

2. Click the Mark Favorite button or press F (**Figure 9.20**). A green bar appears at the top of the filmstrip.

To unmark video:

1. If you changed your mind about some favorited footage, select it.

2. Click the Unmark Selection button, or press U. The green bar disappears from that section.

To reject footage:

1. In the Event Browser, select a range of video you want to reject (**Figure 9.21**).

2. Click the Reject Selection button, or press R. Or, press the Delete key. That footage is hidden (but not permanently deleted).

To control which clips are visible in the Event Browser:

◆ From the Show popup menu at the bottom of the screen, choose one of the options (**Figure 9.22**). Only those clips appear in the browser.

Mark as Favorite

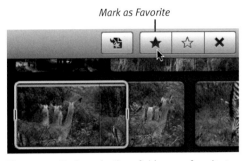

Figure 9.20 Mark a selection of video as a favorite to find it easily when you assembly your movie.

Reject Selection

Figure 9.21 Click the Reject Selection button to hide the selected footage from view (top). You can see that the clip is now shorter based on the length of the green favorite bar (bottom). When you position the mouse over the clip, you would also see that the clip's duration has changed.

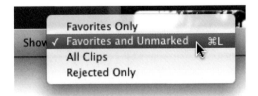

Figure 9.22 Choose an option from the Show popup menu to narrow the options shown.

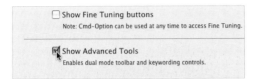

Figure 9.23 Unlock advanced tools from within iMovie's preferences.

Arrow tool   Keyword tool

Figure 9.24 These options dictate what happens when you single-click a clip in the Event Browser.

Marking footage as Favorite

Rejecting footage

Figure 9.25 Simply dragging a selection with the advanced Favorite tool makes it a favorite, versus making a selection and then clicking the button. The actions are color-coded to easily show if you're rejecting footage instead (bottom).

Unmark Selection

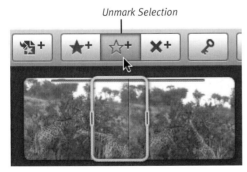

Figure 9.26 If a section of frames is already selected, the toolbar buttons revert to their normal behavior.

Using advanced marking tools

The techniques on the previous page are already more useful than what was offered in earlier versions of iMovie—and yet those represent just the basic marking behavior. Enabling iMovie's advanced tools makes using the marking features faster.

To mark video (advanced):

1. In iMovie's preferences, make sure Show Advanced Tools is enabled (**Figure 9.23**). Two new buttons appear in the toolbar: the Arrow tool and the Keyword tool (**Figure 9.24**).

   The Arrow tool is necessary because the buttons change state. Normally, clicking a button immediately performs an action, but with the advanced tools enabled, clicking a button activates that tool in preparation for the action. So, when you're not using those tools, choose the Arrow tool.

2. Click the Favorite tool, Unmark tool, or Reject tool button to select it.

3. Click and drag across the footage you want to mark (**Figure 9.25**). Continue doing this for every section of video you want to mark or unmark, without switching tools.

✔ Tip

■ When iMovie is in advanced mode and you have a range of video selected, the tool buttons gain a plus sign (**Figure 9.26**). That indicates the buttons work as they do in normal mode: click a button to mark the clip.

Working with Rejected Footage

Remember that iMovie isn't actually deleting any file from your hard disk, only keeping track of which portions of clips have been rejected. You can retrieve the footage at any point, or send it to the Trash if you're sure you won't need it.

To retrieve rejected footage:

1. From the Show menu below the Event Browser, choose Rejected Only. The browser displays only rejected footage with an extra heading titled Rejected Clips (**Figure 9.27**).

2. Select a clip or a range of frames that you want to retrieve.

3. Click the Unmark button.

✔ Tips

■ If you're using advanced mode, click the Unmark button and then drag across the portions you wish to retrieve.

■ You can also retrieve a rejected clip by marking it as a Favorite.

■ Another option is to move footage directly to a Project by clicking the Add to Project button (see the next chapter for more information). When you do this, however, the rejected footage remains marked as rejected; only a copy is sent to the project. Furthermore, when that clip is in a project but the source clip is marked as rejected, iMovie will not move rejected clips to the Trash.

■ Levels of Undo don't transfer between your editing sessions. When you quit iMovie and then launch it again later, your last actions are forgotten.

Figure 9.27 iMovie adds a bright red bar and title in the browser to indicate that this is the reject bin.

Figure 9.28 The original clip on disk, "clip-2005-11-27 11;38;22.dv," was split into three separate clips, but the source file located on the hard disk is not renamed or split.

iMovie File Locations

iMovie HD 6 stored everything—project file, movie clips, title clips—in one *package file* referred to as an iMovie project file. iMovie '08 is less opaque.

You may never need to worry about where the files are located, but if the situation comes up, here's the rundown.

iMovie's files are located in the Movies folder of your Home folder. Inside the Movies folder are three other folders:

- **iMovie Events.** The original movie files you import end up here, within separate folders for each Event (**Figure 9.29**).

- **iMovie Projects.** These are the data files that keep track of which footage is used and which edits are applied.

- **iMovie Sharing.** When you share a movie to iTunes, YouTube, or the Media Browser, the exported versions are stored here.

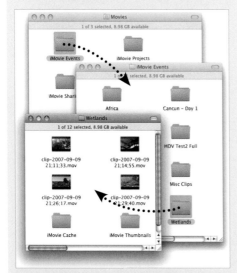

Figure 9.29 Original footage is stored in nested folders based on Event.

How iMovie Manages Clips on Your Hard Disk

At some point you'll decide to really get rid of the rejected clips, not just hide them from view. But before I get into the specifics of sending clips to the Trash on the next page, it's important to understand how iMovie works with the video files stored on your hard disk.

When you import footage, iMovie creates a new clip for each scene, which also adds a new clip file to your hard disk. However, even if you split, duplicate, or otherwise edit a clip in iMovie, *the media file stays the same* (**Figure 9.28**). iMovie actually records only the *changes* made to the clip, and doesn't alter the clip's original media file.

This clip management style comes in handy in several ways as you use iMovie.

Advantages of iMovie's method of managing clips

- **Undo.** iMovie offers virtually unlimited levels of Undo, enabling you to recombine split clips, remove effects that have been applied, and other actions.

- **Deleting clips.** When you trim a clip and throw away one of the portions (described in Chapter 10), that discarded section can be pulled from the piece you kept.

- **Use the same footage in multiple projects.** Add a scene to several movie projects without duplicating the source file on disk. iMovie only needs to reference the original copy.

✔ Tip

- That series of numbers in the media file indicates the date and time the clip was shot. The clip in Figure 9.28 was captured at 11:38:22 a.m. on November 27, 2005 (I guess I'm overdue for another vacation!).

Sending clips to the Trash

If you know (if you're *certain*) you're not going to need any of the deleted clips later, you can move the rejected clips to the Trash. (To be clear, this is the Trash found in the Finder; unlike earlier versions, iMovie '08 does not include an in-program trash.)

To move rejected clips to the Trash:

1. From the File menu, choose Move Rejected Clips to Trash.

2. In the dialog that appears, click the Move to Trash button. If you click View Rejected Clips, iMovie displays only the rejected footage in the Event Browser (as described earlier in this chapter).

   The clip disappears from the Event Browser, and its source file is rewritten so that it contains only the remaining video (**Figure 9.30**).

   Even though the clip seems to be gone from iMovie, however, you can still choose Undo from the Edit menu to bring it back at this point.

3. To free up the space on the hard disk, go to the Finder and choose Empty Trash from the Finder menu. Now it's really gone (well, with one caveat; see the sidebar on the next page).

✔ Tip

- Rather than risk deleting video accidentally, I make a point of never moving rejected footage to the Trash until a project is completely finished—and maybe not even then, if I have enough available disk space.

Figure 9.30 After moving the rejected portion of a clip to the Trash, iMovie rewrites the original file to account for the deleted footage.

Changing Clip Dates and Times

A camcorder marks every clip with the date and time of capture (invisibly, not the little digital clock that appeared on videos of old). But that assumes the camcorder is set with the correct date and time. What if you're working with two video sources (such as a wedding) and one camera's time is off? Since the name of the media file on disk is comprised of just that information, all you have to do is rename the relevant clips.

To change clip dates:

1. Select a clip that needs to be changed in the Event Browser.

2. Right-click or Control-click to bring up the contextual menu and choose Reveal in Finder.

3. Change the date (year-month-day) or time (24-hour format) in the filename. Repeat for other affected clips.

4. Launch iMovie, which rebuilds the clips' thumbnails with the correct information.

WORKING WITH REJECTED FOOTAGE

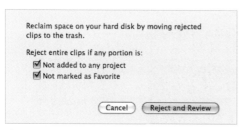

Figure 9.31 Space Saver automates a process that would take too long to do by hand.

Rescuing Clips via Time Machine

If you're running Mac OS X 10.5 Leopard, you have a built-in option for resurrecting clips after you've emptied the Trash. The Time Machine feature backs up any files on your hard disk that have changed in the past hour.

So, although you may have rejected half of a clip, sent it to the Trash, and then emptied the Trash (which rewrites the source clip), the original clip is probably still available.

To restore a clip using Time Machine:

1. Quit iMovie.

2. Click the Time Machine icon in the Dock.

3. Type the name of the clip you're locating in the Finder window's search field. Or, use the timeline at right or the back and forward arrow buttons to browse the save states.

4. When you've found the version of the file you want, select it and click the Restore button. The file is copied to its original folder.

5. Launch iMovie, which will rebuild the Event's thumbnails and include the formerly deleted clip.

Using iMovie's Space Saver

We're jumping ahead a little here, but when you've finished editing a project you can use iMovie's Space Saver feature to remove footage and reduce clutter in the Event Library.

To remove footage using Space Saver:

1. Select one or more events you want to clean up in the Event list.

2. Choose Space Saver from the File menu.

3. In the dialog that appears, choose which types of footage are to be moved to the Trash: video that doesn't appear in any projects and video that's currently unmarked (**Figure 9.31**).

4. Click the Reject and Review button to continue. iMovie displays the Rejected Clips view in the Event Browser so you can double-check which clips are going to be deleted.

5. Click Move Rejected to Trash to delete the clips from the Event Library.

✔ Tips

- Don't forget that even if you empty the Trash, you still have a backup of your clips: the original footage stored on your camcorder's tape.

- No doubt about it, video takes up a lot of disk space. If you don't mind a slight reduction in quality, an interesting utility called iMovie '08 Library Compressor (inik.net/node/168) can re-encode your imported DV footage to MPEG-4 format.

- If you're not running Leopard, or don't use Time Machine, a regular backup system should enable you to restore files that have been deleted. See Joe Kissell's *Take Control of Mac OS X Backups* (www.takecontrolbooks.com/backup-macosx.html).

Assigning Keywords

Figure 9.32 The Keyword tool appears when Show Advanced Tools is enabled in iMovie's preferences.

One curious omission in iMovie '08 was the capability to name clips, a feature in previous versions that helped you determine what scenes a clip contained. The filmstrip and skimming made naming clips mostly unnecessary. However, you don't necessarily want to search your entire Event Library visually.

iMovie's keyword feature goes far beyond naming clips. Keywords are part of iMovie's advanced tools, so if you're not seeing the options I describe here, make sure the Show Advanced Tools option is enabled in iMovie's preferences.

To assign keywords using Auto-Apply:

1. Click the Keyword tool or press K to bring up the Keyword window, and click the Auto-Apply button if it's not already selected (**Figure 9.32**).

2. Select the checkboxes of the keywords you want to apply (**Figure 9.33**). You can also enable or disable them quickly by pressing the numbers 1 through 9 (keywords in the slots for 10 and above don't get keyboard shortcuts).

3. In the Event Browser, drag to select the range of frames to which you want to assign the keywords (**Figure 9.34**). A blue line appears in the filmstrip to indicate where keywords are applied.

To assign keywords using the Keywords Inspector:

1. Taking the opposite approach, first use the Arrow tool to select a range of frames you want to tag with keywords.

2. Click the Keyword tool (or press K); the Inspector button is already selected.

3. Click keywords to apply them (or press their number key equivalents).

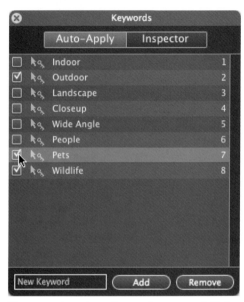

Figure 9.33 A number of keywords are set up initially to get you started.

Figure 9.34 As with marking favorites or rejects in advanced mode, drag to apply keywords to selected footage.

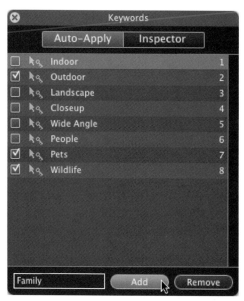

Figure 9.35 Create keywords that reflect the content of your own footage.

Figure 9.36 iMovie keeps track of which keywords have been applied.

Figure 9.37 Keywords appear at the bottom of the Playhead Info display.

To create a new keyword:

1. Type a word or phrase into the New Keyword field.

2. Click the Add button, or press Return (**Figure 9.35**). The keyword appears in the list.

To remove keywords:

1. Click to select one or more keywords in the list.

2. Click the Remove button. If the keyword has been applied to footage, iMovie verifies that you want to remove it from the clips (**Figure 9.36**). Click Yes.

To rename keywords:

1. Double-click a keyword in the list.

2. Type a new keyword in its place. If the keyword has been applied, iMovie asks if you want to change it. Click Yes.

✔ Tips

■ Rearrange the entries in the Keywords Inspector by dragging them up or down in the list.

■ To see which keywords are applied to a clip, choose Playhead Info from the View menu. The keywords appear in addition to the capture date and time (**Figure 9.37**).

■ If you think you'll use only a few keywords, delete the others and keep your list at nine items or less. Then you can use the number keys to apply keywords without even looking at the Keyword window.

ASSIGNING KEYWORDS

Viewing clips according to keywords

Once you've assigned keywords to your clips, it's much easier to locate just the footage you need.

To filter the Event Browser by keyword:

1. Display the Keyword Filter pane by choosing Keyword Filter from the Window menu, or by clicking the Keyword Filter button that becomes visible when you enable advanced tools (**Figure 9.38**).

2. Enable the checkboxes for keywords you want to filter against.

3. Choose a filtering logic (**Figure 9.39**):

   ▲ **Any** applies the filter to any clip with that keyword.

   ▲ **All** applies the filter only to clips that contain all of the keywords that are selected.

   ▲ **Include** instructs iMovie to *show* just the clips with the applicable keywords.

   ▲ **Exclude** *hides* clips that contain the selected keywords.

✔ Tips

- When you hide the Keyword Filter pane, the filtering no longer applies.

- After keywords are set up, you can turn off the advanced mode and still filter your footage. The keywords no longer show up in the Playhead Info display and the blue bars disappear. However, you can still view the Keyword Filter pane (choose Keyword Filter from the Window menu) and apply the filtering logic.

Keyword Filter pane button

Figure 9.38 The Keyword Filter pane provides another level of choosing which clips will appear.

No filter applied   People keyword

"People" clips excluded

"People" clips included

Figure 9.39 Selecting the People keyword with the selectors set to *exclude any* causes the clip of the man (top) to disappear (middle). Setting it to include results in just the People clips appearing (bottom).

Figure 9.40 Betcha never expected to see a Print dialog in iMovie.

Printing an Event

Print? As in, on paper? Aren't we dealing with *video* here? While printing almost sounds like an outdated concept, iMovie offers the capability to make a hard copy version of an Event's footage for people who prefer to review information on paper.

To print an Event:

1. Select one or more items in the Event list.

2. Choose Print Event from the File menu, or press Command-P. The Print dialog appears (**Figure 9.40**).

3. In the iMovie portion of the dialog, choose a preferred number of pages, which dictates the size of the filmstrip thumbnails.

4. If you want to be able to see keywords and clip markings, enable the Show metadata checkbox.

5. Click Print to send the job to your printer. The end result uses the Event Browser's view settings (such as thumbnail size and number of thumbnails per second) to generate the printout (**Figure 9.41**).

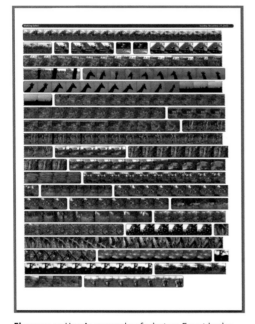

Figure 9.41 Here's a sample of what an Event looks like printed, in this case with the clip size slider set to 1s (1 second) and the thumbnail size slider set at about 25 percent of full size.

10

EDITING VIDEO

The first movies were pure documentaries. Armed with new technology, camera operators shot what they saw: trains leaving the station, people at work, the movement of animals. Motion pictures didn't need to tell a story because the story was in the reproduction. The first movie created by brothers Louis and Auguste Lumière was the action spectacular *Workers Leaving the Lumière Factory*, depicting exactly that.

However, filmmakers soon realized that their "flickers" didn't need to be just linear slices of life. They could shoot movies in any order and assemble them to tell a story, or even combine totally unrelated scenes for dramatic effect. Lev Kuleshov, an early Russian filmmaker, filmed a closeup of an actor wearing a neutral expression. He then intercut a scene of an empty bowl, prompting audiences to praise the actor's subtle portrayal of hunger. Kuleshov took the same neutral footage and intercut scenes of a dead woman in a coffin, then a girl playing with a doll, and in each case audiences were amazed to see the actor's grief or joy. Editing became a vehicle for expressing emotions or ideas that weren't necessarily present during filming.

Today, iMovie and non-linear editing give you the capability to use the visual language of film to tell stories, whether fiction or simply a day at the park. The fun begins here!

Time and Timecode

In Chapter 2, I explained how timecode works as it applies to a camcorder. In iMovie, time is displayed as fractions of seconds by default. If you're more comfortable with traditional timecode, which expresses individual frames instead of seconds, you can switch to that display. Either way, you'll find time displayed in several areas.

To enable timecode display:

1. Choose Preferences from the iMovie menu to open the preferences window, or press Command-, (comma).

2. Select the Display Timecodes checkbox, then close the window.

Time and Timecode in iMovie

◆ **At the Playhead (Project Browser).** When the Playhead Info display is active (choose Playhead Info from the View menu), it always shows the time relative to the entire movie in your project. So, for example, positioning the Playhead two seconds into a clip that appears in the middle of your movie displays something like "8:14" (in seconds) or "0:08:04" (in timecode) instead of "2s" or "0:02:00" (**Figure 10.1**).

◆ **Beneath the Project Library and the Event Library.** In addition to showing timecode of individual clips, the total length of a project or Event appears below the relevant browser (**Figure 10.2**).

◆ **With a selection.** When you drag to select a range of frames, iMovie displays the duration next to the selection box as well as below the browser (**Figure 10.3**).

Playhead location in Playhead Info display

Figure 10.1 The playhead display refers to time location within the context of the movie, not within the clip. Time is shown here in seconds.

Total movie length   *Playhead location*

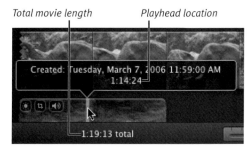

Figure 10.2 The duration of the filmstrip appears below the browser (the Project Library, in this case). Time is shown here in timecode.

Selection relative to total   *Selection duration*

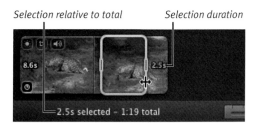

Figure 10.3 Selecting a range of frames offers more information.

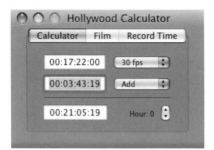

Figure 10.4 Hollywood Calculator is a free tool for handling timecode math.

✔ Tips

- When you select multiple clips, their combined duration appears below the browser.

- Need to quickly figure out the total length of your movie if you add a 3:43:19 clip to it? Plug it into Hollywood Calculator (www.happypixelstudios.com/hwcalc/), a free utility (**Figure 10.4**). Timecode math has never been easier.

- See "Understanding Timecode" in Chapter 2 for a timecode refresher.

Working through the Video Editing Backlog

One of the most common laments among home videographers is the backlog of footage that piles up, unedited. It's easy to shoot hours of video of your kids or vacation, but editing it into movies takes even more hours. I know people who have so many filled MiniDV tapes that they end up not editing any of it because the task is so huge.

The trick is to break the editing down into smaller components, so that it's not such an intimidating endeavor. Instead of facing an entire video that needs to be finished, approach the process in steps. You can tackle a step each weekend, for example. Here's one suggested approach.

1. In the Event Library, delete any full clips you know you won't ever use, such as the times when you didn't know the camera was on (yep, everyone does it). Don't try to edit out portions of clips; this step is just to remove the obvious deadwood.

2. Assemble a rough cut by dragging clips from the Event Browser to the Project Browser in the approximate order you want them to appear in the movie.

3. Start culling the obviously useless footage from your clips using the techniques described in this chapter.

4. Tighten your movie by trimming clips, paying attention to how it's paced. Start adding music and other additional audio.

5. With a tight edit in place, start applying transitions, titles, and effects.

6. Wrap up any final trimming and polishing.

See, it's not that intimidating after all!

TIME AND TIMECODE

Creating a New Project

Just as all of your video footage appears in the Event Library, the movies you create in iMovie all appear in the Project Library—each project is its own movie. When you first launch iMovie, an empty project (My First Project) is already set up; you can jump to the next page if you want to start building your movie in that project. When the time comes to create other movies, follow the steps below.

To create a new project:

1. Choose New Project from the File menu, click the New Project button, or press Command-N (**Figure 10.5**).

2. In the dialog that appears, type a name for the project.

3. Choose an aspect ratio for the project from the popup menu (**Figure 10.6**). Typically this would match the aspect ratio of the shot footage, but if you're going to mix formats or you want to turn your standard video into a widescreen movie, choose the ratio that you want the final movie to be.

4. Click the Create button. The new project appears in the Project list.

To delete a project:

1. Select a project in the Project list.

2. Choose Move Project to Trash from the File menu, or press Command-Delete. The project is moved to the Trash in the Finder.

✔ Tip

■ Since deleting a project moves it to the Finder's Trash, you can easily pull it out later (if you haven't emptied the Trash). Put the project file into the appropriate iMovie Projects folder in the Movies folder within your Home folder, and restart iMovie.

New Project button

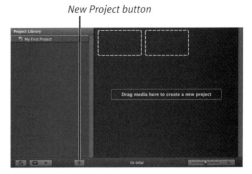

Figure 10.5 All of your movies appear in the Project list, starting with an empty one Apple provides.

Figure 10.6 Choose an aspect ratio for the movie.

Projects Intended for iPhone

You can share a movie of any size to an iPhone, but you'll likely end up with black bars around the edges of the picture to account for the iPhone screen's 3:2 aspect ratio. If you know you want the primary version of your movie to end up on an iPhone or iPod touch, choosing iPhone when you create the project ensures that the movie will use the most screen real estate possible on the device.

CREATING A NEW PROJECT

Add Selection to Project button

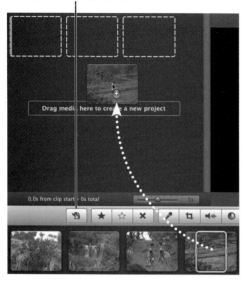

Figure 10.7 Add the footage to your project by dragging it to the Project Browser or clicking the Add Selection to Project button. (Me, I prefer to press E.)

Footage added to project

Clip in Event Browser indicates which footage is being used in a project.

Figure 10.8 Congratulations, you've just created a movie!

Figure 10.9 With the advanced tools enabled, just drag over your chosen footage to add it to the movie.

Adding Clips to the Movie

Even with lots of clips in the Event Library, your movie doesn't exist until you begin building it in the Project Browser.

To add clips to the movie:

1. Select one or more clips or range of footage in the Event Browser.

2. Do one of the following:
   ▲ Drag the selection to the Project Browser (**Figure 10.7**).
   ▲ Click the Add button or press the E key.

   The footage appears in your project's filmstrip (**Figure 10.8**). In the Event Browser, the section of video you added is indicated by an orange bar so you can quickly see which clips are used in a movie.

3. Add more clips to fill out a rough assembly of your movie.

To add clips (advanced mode):

1. Click the Edit tool (normally the Add Selection to Project button) or press E.

2. Drag to select the range of frames that will appear in the project (**Figure 10.9**). The selection appears as a new clip when you release the mouse button.

✔ Tips

- Option-click a clip with the Edit tool selected (in advanced mode) to add an entire clip to the movie.

- Command-click a clip in advanced mode to add just a four second portion of the clip (the default duration can be set in iMovie's preferences).

- If you marked favorite scenes (see the last chapter), choose Favorites Only from the Show popup menu, select all clips in the Event Browser, and then add them at once.

Ordering Clips

The movie's order progresses from left to right, top to bottom (like reading a book) in the Project Browser. You can drag and drop clips into whatever order you choose.

To order clips:

1. Select a clip.

2. Drag the selection to a new location within the filmstrip. Depending on where you release the mouse button, one of two things happens:

   ▲ When you drag to the space between clips, a green bar appears to indicate the point at which the clip will end up (**Figure 10.10**).

   ▲ If you release the mouse when the playhead is in the middle of a clip, that clip is split and your footage appears between the breaks (**Figure 10.11**).

✔ Tips

■ You can only reorder full clips in the Project Browser, not sections of clips. This limitation is easily worked around by editing the clip you want to move (detailed in the next several pages). However, at this point in the editing process, don't get hung up on moving individual sections of clips; you're working in broad strokes for now.

■ You can also copy or cut a selected clip, move the playhead to a new location, and paste the clip. See "Copying and pasting clips," later in this chapter.

■ As editor, you have power over time. Clips can appear in any order, no matter when the events happened chronologically. (Most studio movies are rarely—if ever— shot in chronological order.)

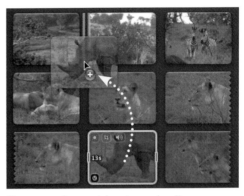

Figure 10.10 Drag and drop to reorder clips.

Playhead in middle of clip

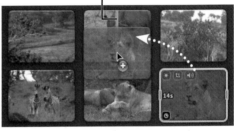

Clip is split after reorder.

Figure 10.11 Dropping into the middle of a clip splits it into two separate clips.

Clip Duration button

Figure 10.12 Click the Clip Duration button to open what Apple calls the "trimmer" (which sounds to me like an exercise machine, but they didn't ask me).

Hidden footage   Play

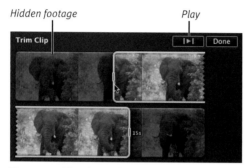

Figure 10.13 The trimmer lets you see an entire clip to better view how the edits apply.

Non-Destructive Editing

In iMovie, clips are *non-destructive*. If you delete a few seconds from the end of a clip, then later decide you need that footage, it's still available to you.

Think of trimming as working with a page of rolled-up blueprints. If you want to view just one portion of the plans, you roll the edges in to hide the rest of the design. In an iMovie video clip, you can hide the frames you choose not to use in your movie. If you need those frames later, you can simply unroll the edges of the clip to display the footage.

Editing Clips

Remember in Chapter 2 when I advised you to shoot plenty of footage? Take a moment to look back on those lingering, leisurely days, because in this chapter you're going to chop your film into the smallest pieces you can, and still keep it comprehensible. Part of your job as editor is to arrange the many pieces into a unified whole, but you also want to keep your audience awake.

Trimming

In the days of editing film, scenes would be shortened by literally trimming the excess frames with a razor blade. The same idea still applies digitally, though you won't need to dig around in a large trim bin (basically a laundry bin filled with celluloid) to find excised footage later.

Several trimming techniques are available: the trimmer presents an overview approach, but you can edit more quickly by cropping or deleting selections.

To trim a clip using the trimmer:

1. In the Project Browser, position the mouse pointer over the clip you want to edit.

2. Click the Clip Duration button (**Figure 10.12**), choose Trim from the Edit menu, or press Command-R. The Project Browser disappears to make way for the trimmer.

3. Drag the left and right edges to define the clip's start and end points (**Figure 10.13**). The frames within the yellow selection box remain visible in your movie, while the dimmed areas outside the selection are hidden.

   To preview the selection in the Viewer, click the Play button.

4. Click the Done button when finished. The clip in the Project Browser is made up only of the visible frames.

To adjust a trim edit:

1. If you want to recover some of those hidden frames, click the Clip Duration button, which opens the trimmer.

2. Move the start or end point to change the length of the visible clip.

If you want to change the start and end points without altering the clip's duration, click and drag in the middle of the selection to re-center the selection (also known as a slip edit, **Figure 10.14**).

3. Click Done when you're finished editing.

To crop a clip:

1. Select a portion of a clip.

2. Choose Trim to Selection from the Edit menu, or press Command-B. The selection is retained, and the rest of the clip's frames are deleted (**Figure 10.15**).

To delete frames from within a clip:

1. Select a portion of a clip.

2. Choose Cut or Delete Selection from the Edit menu, or press the Delete key. The selection is removed, leaving the rest of the footage as two clips (**Figure 10.16**).

If you chose to cut the selection, it will be stored in the Mac's Clipboard.

✔ Tips

■ For more control when dragging the edges of the selection in the trimmer, adjust the thumbnail slider to a lower value such as 1/2s (one half second).

■ To adjust the start and end points in one-frame increments in the trimmer, place the pointer near the edge you want to edit. Hold the Option key and press the left or right arrow keys; the Viewer displays the first or last visible frame, depending on which edge you're adjusting.

Selection re-centered

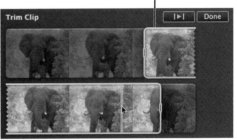

Figure 10.14 Compare the position of this selection with Figure 10.13 to see how the start and end points have changed but not the duration.

Selection made

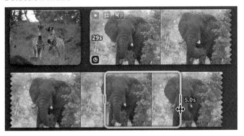

After applying Trim to Selection

Figure 10.15 Cropping removes the footage on either side of the selection.

Previous location of deleted footage

Figure 10.16 When you delete the selected footage, the remaining sections become two clips.

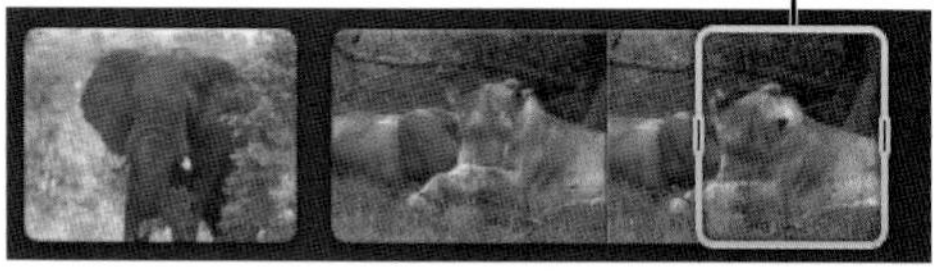

Selection made

Figure 10.17 Splitting a clip in iMovie '08 requires that you make a selection based on the split point.

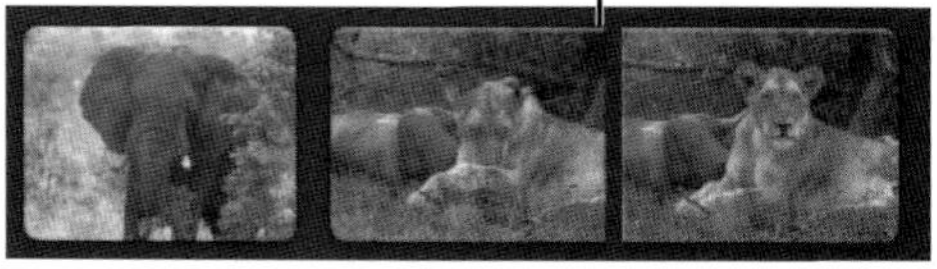

Straight corner indicates clip is split.

Figure 10.18 A split clip acts like two separate clips, but the corners reveal that the clip has been split.

Selecting the middle of a clip

Clip split

Figure 10.19 Splitting a clip from the middle results in three pieces.

Moving Split Clips

As long as the pieces of a split clip remain positioned next to one another, iMovie treats them as split. If you move one segment, the split pieces are considered separate clips. But if you move them back into the proper order, they become split pieces again.

Splitting clips

iMovie can also split clips, which lets you break a clip into smaller pieces without deleting (hiding) any of its footage.

To split a clip:

1. Position the pointer over the frame where you want the split to occur and then select to the end of the clip (**Figure 10.17**).

2. Choose Split Clip from the Edit menu. A new clip is created and placed next to the original (**Figure 10.18**).

To join split clips:

1. Press Shift and click on any section of the split clip to select it.

2. Choose Join Clip from the Edit menu. The pieces come together again.

✔ Tips

- The editing commands are also available from the contextual menu; Control-click or right-click a selection to access them.

- After you split a clip or delete a section from its middle, each half still contains all of the frames it had when they were one (thanks to iMovie's non-destructive editing). Use the trimmer to reveal the hidden frames.

- In the trimmer, press the left or right arrow keys to move (slip) the entire selection in one-frame increments.

- If you make a selection in the middle of a clip and then choose Split Clip, the clip is split into three pieces (**Figure 10.19**).

Copying and pasting clips

Don't forget the tried-and-true method of copying a clip or some footage and pasting it elsewhere in the filmstrip.

To copy and paste footage:

1. Select a clip or a portion of a clip.

2. Choose Copy from the Edit menu, or press Command-C. The selection is stored in your Mac's Clipboard.

3. Position the Playhead in your movie to the location where you want the clip to appear, then choose Paste from the Edit menu (Command-V). iMovie inserts the new clip at that point, splitting any clip that was present and pushing its remaining footage to the right (**Figure 10.20**).

To duplicate a clip by Option-dragging:

1. Select a clip or a portion of a clip.

2. Option-drag the clip to an empty space in the filmstrip (**Figure 10.21**).

Fine tuning edits

The techniques described thus far are, in general, broad edits designed to chop away unneeded footage in seconds and fractions of seconds. But unless you've set the thumbnail slider way down to 1/2s, it's hard to edit at the frame level. That's where fine tuning comes in.

To enable fine tuning:

1. Choose Preferences from the iMovie menu, or press Command-, (comma).

2. Mark the checkbox labeled Show Fine Tuning buttons (**Figure 10.22**), and then close the Preferences window. The buttons appear in the lower corners of the clip (**Figure 10.23**).

Figure 10.20 After copying a portion of the top-left clip, I pasted it into the middle of the next clip. Doing so broke the second clip into two clips.

Figure 10.21 Hold Option and drag to duplicate a clip.

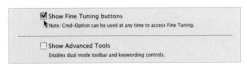

Figure 10.22 The Show Fine Tuning buttons option in preferences makes the controls always visible.

Fine tune start button   *Fine tune end button*

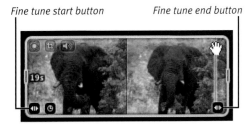

Figure 10.23 The Fine Tuning buttons appear at the bottom edges of each clip.

Figure 10.24 Clicking the Fine Tuning button.

This edit is revealing 17 hidden frames and extending the clip to 20 seconds.

Figure 10.25 Drag to edit in one-frame increments.

Get In, Get Out

There are times when long, lingering shots can define a scene or even an entire movie—but not many. When you're editing, concentrate on making your movies *tight*, showing only the essential shots within your scenes. For example, it's a good idea to have an establishing shot of a room, and perhaps a person opening the door. But you don't need to show him closing the door, walking to the center of the room, and beginning a conversation. Jump right to the conversation, since that's probably the core action of the scene. This advice applies to all types of movies: for your trip to the zoo, jump straight to the lions; we don't need to see you bounce along the pathway looking for directions.

Of course, there are always exceptions (watching *2001: A Space Odyssey* immediately comes to mind), but a tighter film is almost always a better film.

To apply fine-tune edits (the slow way):

1. Move your pointer over the clip you want to edit and click one of the Fine Tuning buttons, depending on whether you want to edit the start or end of the clip. The clip border becomes orange and the adjoining clip moves out of the way to give you some working room (**Figure 10.24**).

2. Drag the edge handle left or right to hide or restore up to one second of footage (30 frames for NTSC, 25 frames for PAL) (**Figure 10.25**). Keep an eye on the Viewer to see the current frame as you drag.

3. Release the mouse button when you've reached the frame you want.

    To fine tune beyond one second, repeat steps 1 and 2 (or perform a trim edit and then fine tune that).

To apply fine-tune edits (the fast way):

◆ Instead of enabling the Fine Tuning buttons at all, simply hold down the Command and Option keys when the pointer is near the edge of a clip. The border turns orange and you can then make a frame-by-frame edit by dragging the edge.

To apply fine-tune edits (the really fast way):

◆ Position the pointer near the edge you want to edit, hold down Option, and press the left or right arrow key.

Cropping and Rotating

The downside to iMovie's capability to mix and match formats and aspect ratios is making them play nice in the same frame. Importing widescreen footage into a standard DV project, for example, results in black bars above and below the image to occupy the unused space (called *letterboxing*).

iMovie '08 gives you the option of cropping footage to use the entire screen (or even eliminate a portion of a scene) or of fitting the entire clip into the frame with black bars.

To crop a clip:

1. Click the Crop button on the clip you want to adjust (**Figure 10.26**). You can also click the Crop button in the toolbar and then select a clip.

   The clip's thumbnail displays a thin yellow border and a circle within the playhead; position the playhead and it will stick (skimming is turned off).

2. In the Viewer, click the Crop button. iMovie displays a highlighted region that matches the project's aspect ratio (**Figure 10.27**).

3. To reposition the cropping region, click within it and drag. To change the size of the region, drag a corner handle; the aspect ratio remains consistent. You can resize the region down to 50 percent of the original size (**Figure 10.28**).

4. Click the Play button to preview the cropped clip in the Viewer. Click Done when you're finished editing.

✔ Tip

■ Resizing a crop region decreases the video resolution. If you're starting with high-def footage you may not notice, but resizing standard DV can get fuzzy.

Crop button   Position playhead

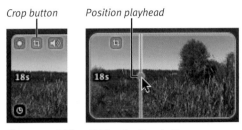

Figure 10.26 After clicking the Crop button, you can position the playhead, where it will remain in place.

Figure 10.27 iMovie crops the widescreen clip so that the image fills the project's aspect ratio.

Figure 10.28 The crop region has been resized and moved to focus on a specific area of the video.

CROPPING AND ROTATING

Rotate counter-clockwise   *Rotate clockwise*

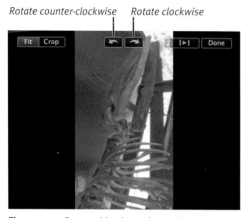

Figure 10.29 Rotate video in 90-degree increments.

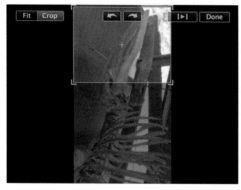

Figure 10.30 To account for the change in aspect ratio, you may want to crop the rotated image.

Figure 10.31 After rotating and cropping, the clip fills the entire screen when played back.

To fit a clip:

1. Click the Crop button in a clip.

2. In the Viewer, click the Fit button. The video appears with black bars to fill out the project's aspect ratio.

If you've previously applied a crop, click the Fit button to revert back to the clip's original aspect ratio.

3. Click Done when you're finished.

Rotating clips

In Chapter 2, I mentioned that some people use a camcorder like a still camera and rotate it to take vertical shots. If you find yourself with scenes like that, or you want to just rotate your video for your own entertainment, here's how to do it.

To rotate a clip:

1. Click the Crop button in a clip.

2. Click one of the rotation buttons to rotate the clip 90 degrees clockwise or counter-clockwise (**Figure 10.29**).

3. Because the rotated clip won't match the project's aspect ratio, optionally click Crop to fill the frame with the image (**Figure 10.30**).

4. Click Done when you're finished. The rotated clip looks like you shot it that way (**Figure 10.31**).

✔ Tips

- Specify whether clips are automatically cropped or sized to fit. Choose File > Project Properties and change the Initial Video Placement setting.

- When you're cropping a clip, you can click other clips to apply cropping without clicking the Done button each time.

CROPPING AND ROTATING

Making Video Adjustments

The best thing you can do to improve the quality of your video is to shoot good quality footage. And while that's a noble goal, it's just not always possible—your camera didn't adjust its white point correctly, the day was too cloudy, you forgot to hire a director of photography for your multimillion-dollar major studio picture....

As you might expect, iMovie's adjustments aren't nearly up to the same quality as the tools found in Final Cut Studio, but they can be pretty useful for tweaking color or lightening a dark scene.

To adjust color:

1. Click the Video Adjustments button in the clip you want to edit (**Figure 10.32**), or click the Video Adjustments button in the toolbar and select the clip.

2. Use any of the following controls (**Figure 10.33**) to change the look of the footage previewed in the Viewer.

   ▲ **Auto.** Click this button to let iMovie calculate the best settings.

   ▲ **Levels.** The histogram at the top of the window represents the levels of red, blue, and green in the current frame. The sliders below the graph represent the darkest and lightest values (pure black or white).

   Drag the left slider toward the middle to darken the image; drag the right slider similarly to lighten the image. Doing so treats the furthermost colors on the outside edges as darkest or lightest (**Figure 10.34**).

   ▲ **Exposure.** This slider brightens or darkens the video's highlights.

   ▲ **Brightness.** This slider controls the overall lightness of the clip.

Video Adjustments button

Figure 10.32
The Video Adjustments button indicates whether adjustments are applied. Click it to open the Video Adjustments window.

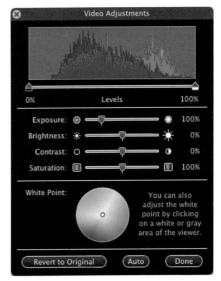

Figure 10.33 A selection of color enhancement tools are available to adjust your video.

Figure 10.34 The levels in the original video (left) are fairly well balanced. Drastically moving the white-point slider brightens the image far too much (right).

MAKING VIDEO ADJUSTMENTS

Figure 10.35 The White Point setting often warms up cloudy day footage that would otherwise be drab.

Figure 10.36 Making video black and white is simply a matter of eliminating the color saturation.

Figure 10.37 Create a sepia tone by manipulating the percentages in the gain sliders.

▲ **Contrast.** Accentuate the differences between light and dark.

▲ **Saturation.** Drag this slider to change the color intensity.

▲ **White Point.** This control tells iMovie which color value equals white; the rest of the colors are based on that value. Move the point within the color wheel to adjust the white point, which can also affect the clip's color cast (**Figure 10.35**). Or, click within the Viewer to specify which color should be treated as white (it also bases its settings on gray values).

▲ **Revert to Original.** If you don't like the adjustments you made, click here to go back to the original settings.

3. When you're finished making adjustments, click the Done button.

To make video black and white:

1. Select a clip and bring up the Video Adjustments window.

2. Set the Saturation slider all the way left to zero (**Figure 10.36**).

To manipulate red, green, and blue colors (advanced mode):

1. In iMovie's preferences, enable Show Advanced Tools.

2. Bring up the Video Adjustments window.

3. Move the Red Gain, Green Gain, and Blue Gain sliders to adjust those colors.

✔ Tip

■ To give your footage a sepia tone, set the Saturation slider to zero and set the gain sliders to the following: Red Gain: 143%; Green Gain: 89%; Blue Gain: 53% (**Figure 10.37**). (And feel free to adjust those as you see fit.)

Copying and Pasting Adjustments

When you make adjustments, the settings are applied to the entire clip. If other clips in your movie were shot at the same time (or you just want the same adjustments), you can apply the same settings without having to duplicate them one by one.

To copy and paste video adjustments:

1. Select a clip that has adjustments applied.

2. Choose Copy from the Edit menu or from the contextual menu, or press Command-C.

3. Select the clip (or clips) to which you want to apply the adjustments.

4. Go to the Edit menu, highlight the Paste Adjustments submenu, and choose Video (or press Command-Option-I) (**Figure 10.38**).

   This technique also applies to pasting cropping and audio adjustments, too.

✔ Tips

- Video adjustments can be applied to clips in either the Project Browser or the Event Browser.

- Filmstrip thumbnails don't display video adjustments—for example, a black and white clip still appears in color in the browsers (**Figure 10.39**). Skim over the clip to see how it appears in the Viewer.

- You'll probably use the Video Adjustments window to tweak colors or exposure, but remember that you can do some serious damage to your image—and I mean that in a good way. Don't hesitate to crank the sliders when a scene calls for odd visuals. It's all digital, and you won't *actually* damage the video: the original remains untouched on your hard disk.

Figure 10.38 Once you apply a set of adjustments, you can paste them to other clips and save yourself some repetitive work.

Figure 10.39 This clip has been made black and white in the Video Adjustments window, but its thumbnail still appears in color in the Project Browser.

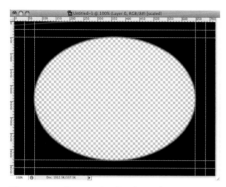

Figure 10.40 I created a simple oval over a transparent background in Photoshop.

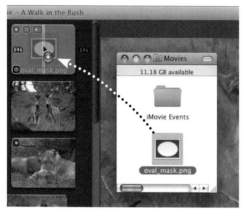

Figure 10.41 Drag the image file from the Finder onto a clip in the Project Browser.

Figure 10.42
The image appears attached above the clip in the Project Browser. The completed effect can be seen in the Viewer (below).

Masking Video

People accustomed to iMovie HD were surprised to learn that iMovie '08 doesn't include effects or support for third-party plug-ins. Some of those capabilities moved elsewhere, such as the controls in the Video Adjustments window. But here's a hidden technique that helps make up for the loss of effects. With a little outside help, you can create a mask for your video.

To create a video mask:

1. In an image editor such as Adobe Photoshop, create an image matching the dimensions of your project (**Figure 10.40**). Make sure it's on a separate layer to give it transparency.

2. Save the image as a PNG file with transparency enabled.

3. Drag the image file from the Finder *onto the top of* the clip you want to add it to (**Figure 10.41**). The clip icon turns blue to indicate that you're adding an image to the clip.

   Once added, the mask appears as if it were a title above the clip thumbnail. You can then move the mask or change its duration (**Figure 10.42**).

   This technique also opens up the possibility of adding items to the frame to help visually punctuate ideas, such as title styles not offered by iMovie or photos you want to include but not occupy the entire frame.

✔ Tip

- Credit for this idea enthusiastically goes to Karel Gillissen, by way of the Unlocking iMovie '08 blog (`imovie08.blogspot.com`). Check it out!

Working with Source Clips

It's not uncommon for me to chop up a single long clip into so many little pieces that I've lost track of where they are. Trimming lets you cobble pieces together, but what if you want to just start fresh?

Thanks to the way iMovie stores files, you can recover a pristine version of a clip. Clips you create don't actually exist as new files on your hard disk. Instead, iMovie simply notes what changes have been applied to clips, and grabs the necessary information from the clip's original data file.

To revert a clip:

1. Select a clip in the Project Browser that you want to restore.

2. Control-click to bring up the contextual menu and choose Reveal in Event Browser (**Figure 10.43**). The segment you selected appears highlighted in gray on the source clip.

3. Grab the footage you want from the source clip.

To locate a source file on disk:

1. In either the Project Browser or Event Browser, select a clip and bring up the contextual menu (Control-click).

2. Choose Reveal in Finder. The clip appears selected in a new Finder window (**Figure 10.44**).

Clip segment

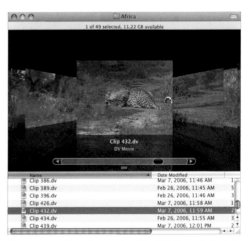

Source clip with segment highlighted

Figure 10.43 Choose Reveal in Event Browser to locate a clip's source.

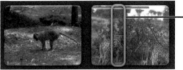

Figure 10.44 If you're running Mac OS X 10.5 Leopard, the Cover Flow view provides easy previews of your source files.

Editing Still Pictures

After purchasing a camcorder, I didn't immediately throw away my trusty digital still camera. In fact, on a day-to-day basis, I find myself taking more photos than shooting video footage; compact digital cameras are just so easy to carry around.

iMovie makes it easy to incorporate those stills into your movie projects, whether you're creating a slideshow, adding a series of pictures to accentuate video footage, or creating graphics or Photoshop-enhanced title screens. With iMovie, it's a snap to add any image from your iPhoto library.

This chapter also includes information about the highly touted Ken Burns Effect, a pan-and-zoom operation that adds motion to otherwise static images.

Importing Pictures from iPhoto

iMovie can easily import photos you've scanned or taken with a digital still camera. iMovie makes this process easier by giving you access to your library of pictures in iPhoto (as well as Aperture and Photo Booth).

To import pictures from iPhoto:

1. Display the Photos Browser by choosing Photos from the Window menu, clicking the Photos button, or pressing Command-2 (**Figure 11.1**).

2. Your entire photo library is shown in the preview area. If you want to access a specific photo album, choose its name from the list. You can also choose Events and browse iPhoto Events by skimming the mouse pointer over them. Double-click an Event to view the photos contained within it.

   Alternately, type a name into the search field to locate pictures based on their titles (**Figure 11.2**).

3. Drag the picture from the Photos Browser to a space between clips in the Project Browser (**Figure 11.4**, opposite).

   The Ken Burns Effect is automatically applied to the photo when it's imported, but you can edit or turn off the effect, as discussed later in this chapter.

✔ Tips

- Double-clicking a photo thumbnail expands it to fit within the preview area to give you a better look at it.

- Command-click to select multiple photos at once, then drag them to the Project Browser to add them as a batch. Dragging an Event also adds all still photos within it. Each photo receives the same duration and Ken Burns Effect settings.

Click other sources in the list.   Photos button

Figure 11.1 All the pictures in your iPhoto library are accessible from within the Photos Browser.

Figure 11.2 Use the search field to quickly locate photos using names you assigned to them in iPhoto.

Photos Browser Display

Drag the thumbnail size slider in the Photos Browser to enlarge or reduce the image thumbnails. You can also drag the divider between the list of sources and the photos; the list becomes a single popup menu and makes more room for images (**Figure 11.3**).

Figure 11.3 The photo sources as a popup menu.

Figure 11.4 Drag a picture from the Photos Browser to the Project Browser to add it to your movie.

Trim icon

Figure 11.5
Click the Trim icon to change a still photo's duration.

Figure 11.6 The duration of still photos can be applied to just one image or to all photos in the project.

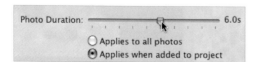

Figure 11.7 Set a default duration in Project Properties.

Changing the Duration of a Still Clip

Although a still clip appears in the filmstrip like any other video clip, iMovie treats it slightly differently. Instead of trimming a photo, you simply change its duration. You can also set a default duration for incoming photos or all photos in a project.

To change a picture's duration:

1. Click the trim icon in the photo's thumbnail (**Figure 11.5**). You can also choose Set Duration from the Edit menu or the contextual menu, or press Command-R.

2. In the Set Duration dialog, enter a new value into the Duration field (**Figure 11.6**).

3. Click one of the radio buttons to specify whether the new duration applies to only the selected photo or to all photos in the project. Click OK to apply the setting.

To set a default photo duration:

1. Choose Project Properties from the File menu or press Command-J.

2. In the dialog that appears, move the Photo Duration slider to set a new default time (**Figure 11.7**).

3. Choose when the duration should apply: either to all photos currently in the project, or when a photo is added. Click OK.

✔ Tips

- If you've selected multiple photos in your project and you choose Applies only to selected photo in the Set Duration dialog, the setting affects only the clip where the playhead currently resides. Other selected clips are unaffected.

- When you change a photo's duration, the Ken Burns Effect adapts to the new length.

Adding Motion with the Ken Burns Effect

Who says still photos must remain still? A common effect used by documentary film-makers is *pan and zoom*, where the camera moves across a still image, zooms in on (or out of) a portion of the image, or performs a combination of the two.

To change whether the Ken Burns Effect is automatically applied:

1. Choose Project Properties from the File menu or press Command-J.

2. From the Initial Photo Placement popup menu (**Figure 11.8**), choose one of the following:

   ▲ **Fit in Frame.** iMovie includes the entire photo, possibly resulting in black bars at the edges to account for the difference in aspect ratios between the photo and project.

   ▲ **Crop.** iMovie fills the frame with the photo.

   ▲ **Ken Burns.** A basic Ken Burns Effect is applied to every new photo added to the project.

3. Click OK to apply the setting, which affects new photos you add (not stills you've already imported).

To edit the Ken Burns Effect:

1. Add a photo to your project. If the Ken Burns Effect was automatically applied, skip to Step 4.

2. Click the photo's Crop icon, which loads the image into the Viewer.

3. Click the Ken Burns button. iMovie applies a basic zoom effect (**Figure 11.9**).

4. Position the effect's starting frame: click the green Start rectangle and move and

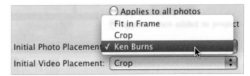

Figure 11.8 Specify how new photos are treated.

Figure 11.9 Ken Burns Effect is applied.

Figure 11.10 The Start frame has been cropped and shifted to the left to accentuate this giraffe's head. The yellow arrow indicates the direction the zoom effect will follow when played back.

Figure 11.11 Now we're setting up the last frame of the effect—zoomed in and shifted to the right.

Start

End

Figure 11.12 The completed Ken Burns Effect zooms out and pans to view all the giraffes.

— *Reverse button*

Figure 11.13 Click the Reverse button to quickly swap the Start and Finish settings.

Ken Who?

Ever one to capitalize on name recognition, Apple named this feature after Ken Burns, a documentary filmmaker who frequently employs the effect in his popular documentaries. Examples include *The Civil War*, *JAZZ*, and *Baseball*. For more information, see www.pbs.org/kenburns/.

resize it (**Figure 11.10**). When played back, the contents of the Start rectangle will fill the window; press the Play button to preview the effect.

5. Set the final frame of the effect by clicking the red End box to select it and then resizing and positioning it (**Figure 11.11**).

6. When the effect is set up to your liking, click Done.

Figure 11.12 approximates the effect as it appears when played back.

To apply the same effect to multiple still photos:

1. After configuring the Ken Burns Effect on one photo, select the clip and choose Copy from the Edit menu to copy its attributes.

2. Select another still photo.

3. Go to the Edit menu and choose Crop from the Paste Adjustments submenu (or press Command-Option-R). The effect is applied.

4. Repeat Steps 2 and 3 for any other photos.

✔ Tips

- If you decide you want your effect to run backwards from the way you set it, click the Reverse button to swap the Start and End settings (**Figure 11.13**).

- The speed of the effect depends on the duration of the clip. For a slower effect, increase the photo's duration.

- For much more control over pan-and-zoom effects, look to Photo to Movie (lqgraphics.com/software/), which gives you the capability to rotate the camera, and add other photos and audio. You can then export the clip as a video file to be imported into iMovie.

ADDING MOTION WITH THE KEN BURNS EFFECT

Importing Pictures from Other Sources

iMovie can easily import photos you've scanned or taken with a digital still camera—or better, images that you've modified in an image-editing program such as Adobe Photoshop (www.adobe.com/products/photoshop/) or GraphicConverter (www.lemkesoft.com).

To import a still picture:

◆ Drag an image file from the Desktop to iMovie's Project Browser (**Figure 11.14**). The photo appears just as you would expect (**Figure 11.15**).

Figure 11.14 Drag an image from the Finder to add it to your project.

Figure 11.15 Come on, did you honestly think I could write an iMovie book and not include a kid's picture?

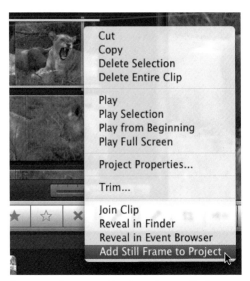

Figure 11.16 Turn any video frame into a still photo.

Figure 11.17 The still frame is added to the end of the project and given the duration specified in the project properties.

Figure 11.18 iMovie creates a new JPEG image for each still you create from video and stores it within the project file.

Creating a Still Clip from a Video Clip

Thousands of still images flicker by as we're watching video—sometimes too quickly. Perhaps you'd like to linger on a sunset or highlight the one short moment when everyone in your family was looking at the camera. You can create a still clip from a single frame of video.

To create a still clip:

1. Position the playhead at the frame you wish to use.

2. Hold Control and click to bring up the contextual menu, and then choose Add Still Frame to Project (**Figure 11.16**). A new still photo clip appears at the end of your project's filmstrip (**Figure 11.17**).

✔ Tips

- Once the still has been created, it's treated like any other still photo, which means you can set up a Ken Burns Effect for it.

- Remember that you're still working in video resolution, so your still clip won't be the same higher-quality that you'd get by taking a photo using a digital still camera.

- To grab that still photo and use it somewhere else (such as adding it to iPhoto), select the clip and choose Reveal in Finder from the contextual menu (Control-click). The image is stored within the project file on disk (which normally isn't obviously accessible), but getting to it this way lets you copy the JPEG file that iMovie creates (**Figure 11.18**).

Creating an Image Overlay

iMovie contains an undocumented feature that's actually an offshoot of its titling capabilities: you can add a still photo on top of your video footage without breaking up the video. This technique can be useful for when you want to toss in pictures without disrupting the audio from the video currently playing. I touched on this capability in Chapter 10 when explaining how to create a video mask.

To create an image overlay:

1. Open the Photos Browser to access your photos (or find a still image file in the Finder).

2. Drag the photo to the Project Browser and drop it onto an existing video clip. The clip turns blue to indicate that it's holding its breath—err, rather that the incoming image is being treated as a title (**Figure 11.19**). (See Chapter 13 for more on working with titles.)

   After you release the mouse button, the photo appears as a clip above the video (**Figure 11.20**). You can edit its duration by dragging the left or right edge. Click and drag in the middle of the clip to change its position relative to the video.

   iMovie automatically adds a cross-dissolve transition to the beginning and ending of the image (**Figure 11.21**).

✔ Tip

■ Dropping the image onto the middle of a video clip gives it the same duration as the clip. You can also drop it onto the start or end of the video clip to get a shorter duration (**Figure 11.22**).

Figure 11.19 Drop an image onto the top of a video clip to create an overlay.

Figure 11.20 The overlay image appears as a clip on top of the video.

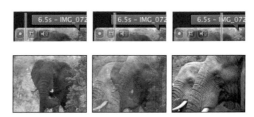

Figure 11.21 The overlay appears with a cross-dissolve transition already in place.

Figure 11.22 Dropping onto the beginning of a clip results in a shorter duration for the overlay.

12

Editing Audio

How important is audio in a movie? If you ever get the chance to attend an advance test screening of a Hollywood movie, the answer may be painfully clear. I've been to screenings where the audio in some scenes consisted of just what was recorded on set—no background music, no sound mixing to balance actors' voices and dampen background noise, no re-recorded dialogue to enhance enunciation. Although quite a bit of work goes into editing audio, people tend not to notice it unless something is wrong.

I covered some methods for capturing quality audio in Chapter 5, which is the first step. But audio can be much more than just video's underappreciated sibling. In this chapter, you'll see how editing audio tracks can give depth to your movie by working independently of the video, and by adding music, narration, and sound effects.

iMovie's New Audio Approach

If you're coming to iMovie '08 from iMovie HD 6, audio editing looks downright perplexing. Audio clips are no longer restricted to just two tracks below the video track, but the new interface makes that difficult to discern. Don't worry, though, it will start to make sense pretty quickly.

Unfortunately, a lot of audio functionality that finally made its way into iMovie HD 6 is absent in iMovie '08. You don't have as much control over audio within a clip, visual waveform display is gone, and the audio effects have also been silenced (including my favorite Noise Reducer).

Hopefully, Apple will roll these functions into later versions of iMovie or open up the program to third-party developers who can restore those functions. In the meantime, you can always export video from iMovie '08, import it into iMovie HD 6, and edit the audio there.

Changing a Clip's Volume

When you import footage, the video and audio are combined in the filmstrip. As you're editing video clips, you're also editing the audio—splitting, trimming, and cropping it with the visuals. You can control how loud an individual clip plays using the Audio Adjustments window.

If there's a lot of variation in the volume of the clips, you can also *normalize* them, which balances each clip to roughly the same level.

To increase or decrease a clip's volume:

1. Select the clip you want to edit in either the Project Browser or the Event Browser and click the Audio Adjustments button in the toolbar. Or, click the button first and then select a clip to edit.

   My preferred option is to click the Audio Adjustments button in the clip's thumbnail (**Figure 12.1**) or just press the A key. The Audio Adjustments window appears.

2. Drag the Volume slider to increase or decrease the clip's volume (**Figure 12.2**).

3. Press the Spacebar to play back the clip, starting at the playhead location. Keep an eye on the volume indicators in the toolbar (**Figure 12.3**). If the levels are pushing into the red zone, your audio is too loud and should be turned down.

To normalize a clip's volume:

1. Select a clip and bring up the Audio Adjustments window.

2. Click the Normalize Clip Volume button. iMovie automatically adjusts the volume. Unfortunately, the only way to tell if a clip has been normalized is to check the thumbnail icon (**Figure 12.4**).

3. Repeat Step 2 on any other clips you want normalized.

Button in clip   Button in toolbar

Figure 12.1 Click one of the Audio Adjustments buttons to edit a clip's audio.

Volume slider

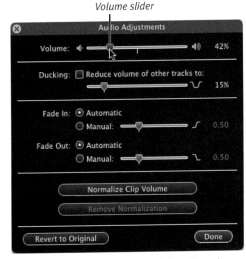

Figure 12.2 Changing the Volume slider affects the audio of an entire clip.

Figure 12.3 The volume indicators make it easy to visually tell if your audio is too loud.

Volume adjusted   Audio normalized

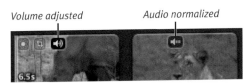

Figure 12.4 Unique icons indicate audio adjustments.

Drag to set duration

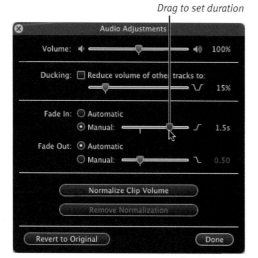

Figure 12.5 You can't specify the amount of fade—it's either silent or whatever is set in the Volume slider—but you can determine how long the fade will last, up to two seconds.

Fading Audio In or Out

One of the more common audio effects is to fade the sound in from silence at the beginning of a scene, or fade it out at the end.

To fade audio in or out:

1. On the clip you want to edit, click the Audio Adjustments button.

2. Drag the slider to set the duration of the fade. For example, to start the clip silent and bring it to full volume over the course of 1.5 seconds, drag the slider to the 1.5s mark (**Figure 12.5**).

3. Click Done to exit the Audio Adjustments window.

✔ Tips

- Moving the Fade In or Fade Out slider enables the Manual radio button; you don't have to click it separately.

- With the tool still selected, you can click another clip and edit its settings without closing the Audio Adjustments window.

- When you apply a Fade In or Fade Out transition (see the next chapter), the audio automatically fades to accompany the visual effect.

- The controls in the Audio Adjustments window apply to audio-only clips (covered in the next several pages) as well as to video clips.

- Unfortunately, the fade controls are amazingly limited, especially if you're used to the freedom afforded by iMovie HD 6. I hope some of the features found in the old version migrate to the new.

Adding Music

I suppose I should have titled this section "Adding Audio Files," but iMovie is really geared toward adding music from iTunes or GarageBand. If you're familiar with other video editing software, one of the first things you may have noticed in iMovie '08 was the lack of distinct audio tracks beneath the video track. It turns out, however, that the tracks are just hidden from view.

iMovie treats music and audio in two ways: Background music literally appears as if it's behind the filmstrip, while other audio clips are attached to the bottom of the filmstrip.

To locate songs in your iTunes or GarageBand libraries:

1. Click the Music and Sound Effects button in the toolbar or choose Music and Sound Effects from the Window menu (or just press Command-1).

2. Click iTunes or GarageBand in the source list. Your library appears in the preview area (**Figure 12.6** and **Figure 12.7**); click the triangle beside either name to view your playlists.

3. Scroll through the list to find the song you want to use.

   Or, type a word in the Search field if you're looking for a particular song or artist name. The list updates as you type (**Figure 12.8**). Click the Cancel button (with the white X on it) to clear the field and return to the full list.

✔ Tips

■ The Search field returns matches for all iTunes metadata, not just titles and artists.

■ Set up a custom iMovie playlist in iTunes that contains the music you want to use for a particular project to help you find songs faster.

Figure 12.6 Narrow your song list by clicking the name of a playlist.

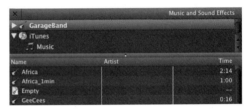

Figure 12.7 When viewing the GarageBand list, the songs with a full guitar icon can be previewed. The songs with document icons must be saved again in GarageBand with an iLife preview before you can play or import them in iMovie.

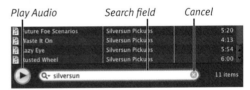

Figure 12.8 Type the name of a song or artist into the Search field to display only the matches in the list.

Figure 12.9 You can also view the song list by icon, which uses the album art (when available).

Figure 12.10 Five columns can be viewed at once.

Artist	Album	Time
Peter Bjorn and John	Writer's Block	0:16
Beirut	The Flying Cl...	0:18
Devotchka	How It Ends	0:25
David Arnold & Nic...	Casino Royal...	0:26
David Arnold & Nic...	Casino Royal...	0:27
David Arnold & Nic...	Casino Royal...	0:27

Figure 12.11 Sorting the library by time makes it easy to find music that matches the length of your video clips or sequences.

Audio Copyright

It's worth pointing out that most songs you import from iTunes are probably copyrighted material. For most people this is no problem, since only friends and family are likely to see their edited movies. But if you're planning to distribute the movie or play it for a lot of people, you need to get permission to use the music.

To add audio files from the Finder:

◆ Drag an audio file from the Finder directly to the Project Browser.

To customize the song list:

◆ Control-click in the song list and choose Display as Icons to view the songs by their album artwork (**Figure 12.9**).

◆ In the list view, Control-click in the song list, go to Show Columns, and choose which columns are visible (**Figure 12.10**).

◆ Click and drag a column heading to change the order in which it appears.

To listen to a song:

1. Select a song in the list.

2. Click the round Play Audio button to play the track from the beginning. Click the button again to stop playing.

✔ Tips

■ Click the column headings to sort the song list (**Figure 12.11**). For example, I often click the Time column to find songs that fit within a given section of a movie.

■ You can make any folder of songs appear in the Audio list: simply drag the folder from the Finder to the top portion of the Media pane. It appears in a Folders folder.

■ iMovie can import any file format that iTunes can play, so you're not limited to just MP3 files.

■ Music encoded in MP3 or AAC format in iTunes is compressed, meaning that some audio data have been removed to make the file size smaller. Most people probably won't notice the difference, but some audiophiles can tell. If you need to use the highest-quality music in your movies, import the songs in AIFF format within iTunes.

ADDING MUSIC

Adding background music

The idea behind background music is that it enables you to quickly throw some tunes behind your video without the hassle of positioning clips on an audio track. iMovie's implementation is a clever interface, though not entirely intuitive if you want to do more with those clips.

To add background music:

1. Drag one or more songs from the song list to a space in the Project Browser that is *outside the filmstrip* (**Figure 12.12**). The background turns green to indicate that you're adding background music.

   When you play your movie, the music plays behind the audio belonging to the video clips.

   If the song file is longer than the movie, it's faded out at the end and marked with a musical note icon to indicate there's more music available (**Figure 12.13**).

2. Drag more music to the background as you see fit. iMovie slots them together so they play consecutively (**Figure 12.14**).

   The clips can be moved and edited in the background; see "Locking Background Audio" and "Trimming Audio Clips," later in this chapter.

To rearrange background music clips:

1. Choose Arrange Music Tracks from the Edit menu. Unlike most objects in iMovie, background audio cannot be rearranged by dragging (as you'll see shortly).

2. In the dialog that appears, ignore the top purple section for now and focus on the lower green section. Click a song title and drag it up or down in the list to change the order (**Figure 12.15**).

3. Click OK to make the change and find the clips repositioned in the Project Browser.

Background music indicator

Figure 12.12 When you drag a song to the area around the filmstrip, it's added as background music.

Figure 12.13 The music note icon tells you that more audio is available, but you're at the end of the video.

First song   Next song

Figure 12.14 A newly-added background song (selected here for emphasis) automatically falls into place after the previous one.

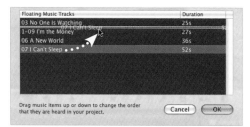

Figure 12.15 Reorder background clips in this dialog.

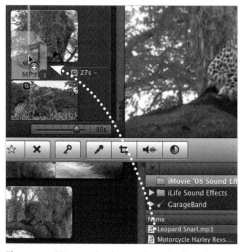

Figure 12.16 For non-background music clips, drag the audio file directly to the filmstrip.

Background music

Audio clip added

Figure 12.17 Audio clips are anchored to the bottom of the video.

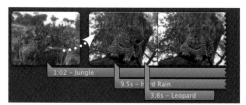

Figure 12.18 So much for the old 2-track limitation.

Adding other audio clips

All other audio clips, such as sound effects, are added to the filmstrip, where they remain anchored.

To add other audio clips:

1. In the Music and Sound Effects Browser, locate the audio clip you'd like to add to the movie. (iMovie '08 includes a set of sound effects that are listed, for example, but you're not limited to effects.)

2. Drag the sound file from the list to the place on the filmstrip where you want the audio to begin (**Figure 12.16**). The Viewer displays the frame beneath the playhead to help you position the clip more accurately.

   The audio clip appears fastened to the bottom of the filmstrip as a green bar (**Figure 12.17**).

   You can continue adding audio clips and—in a change from the past—keep building layers of audio tracks. Simply drag and drop new clips on the filmstrip. iMovie stacks them visually from longest (closest to the filmstrip itself) to shortest to make it obvious where they begin and end (**Figure 12.18**).

To reposition audio clips:

1. Click an audio clip to select it.

2. Drag the clip to a new position. The Viewer displays the frame that corresponds with the beginning of the clip.

✔ Tip

- By default, iMovie snaps the end of an audio clip to edit points such as the beginnings or endings of video and other audio clips. Choose Snap to Ends from the View menu to disable this behavior.

Recording Voiceovers

I read that while shooting *Crouching Tiger, Hidden Dragon*, actor Chow Yun Fat (who doesn't speak Mandarin Chinese natively) didn't put much work into pronouncing his dialogue correctly during filming. Instead, he fine-tuned his accent when re-recording the dialogue in post production. Most likely you won't be doing much re-recording (also called *looping*), but iMovie's narration capability lets you add voiceovers or other sounds directly to your movie.

To record a voiceover:

1. Connect a microphone to your Mac, if necessary.

2. Click the Voiceover button in the toolbar to bring up the Voiceover window (**Figure 12.19**).

3. If you've not already done so, choose an input source from the Record From popup menu.

4. Adjust the Input Volume slider to accommodate for the microphone's sensitivity; if the audio levels are low as you speak, increase the volume percentage, or pull back on the slider if the levels are too high.

5. Set the Noise Reduction slider to filter out ambient noise. You'll record less noise with the slider further to the right.

6. The Voice Enhancement checkbox processes the audio with algorithms geared toward spoken-word recording; uncheck the box if you prefer the sound unprocessed (you'll have to experiment to see which version you prefer).

Voiceover button

Figure 12.19 The Voiceover window displays the current microphone input levels.

Recording started   Current playhead position

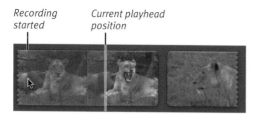

Figure 12.20 The filmstrip turns red to indicate you're currently recording a voiceover.

Voiceover recorded

34s – Voiceover Recording 1

Figure 12.21 When you're finished recording, the voiceover appears as a purple audio clip.

34s – Voiceover Recording 1
4.5s – Voiceover

Figure 12.22 Multiple voiceovers appear as additional audio tracks; delete the ones that didn't turn out well.

7. Enable the last item, Play project audio while recording, if you're listening to the project through headphones and need to pick up audio cues.

8. Click the point on the filmstrip where you want the recording to begin. iMovie counts down 3 seconds before that point and begins recording.

9. Speak into the microphone. The film-strip turns red to indicate where recording has taken place (**Figure 12.20**).

10. Click within the Project Browser, or press the Esc button, to stop recording. A new audio clip, which can be edited just like other audio clips, is now attched to the filmstrip (**Figure 12.21**).

11. To record another voiceover, click another clip. Or, click the Voiceover button in the toolbar again to disable the tool.

To delete a voiceover:

◆ Click a clip to select it, and then press the Delete key or choose Delete Selection from the Edit menu.

✔ Tips

■ You can record multiple takes, then delete the ones you don't end up using (**Figure 12.22**).

■ Some Mac models do not include an audio-in port or a built-in microphone, unfortunately. Instead, consider buying an inexpensive USB audio device such as the iMic, from Griffin Technology (www.griffintechnology.com).

RECORDING VOICEOVERS

Locking Background Audio

Most audio clips are "locked" by default: they remain attached to the point on the filmstrip where you placed them. Background music clips start at the first frame of your movie and are pressed together like cans in a vending machine. However, you can move background audio clips and *pin* (lock) them to a specific frame of video.

Figure 12.23 This background music clip runs after the previous clip, but we want to pin it to the next video clip.

To pin a background audio clip:

1. Click a background audio clip to select it (**Figure 12.23**).

2. Drag the clip to where you want it pinned to the video (**Figure 12.24**). The green floating background audio clip becomes a purple pinned clip that remains attached to that frame of video.

   The oddity in this situation is that any unpinned clips that follow the pinned audio will fill in the gap left open when you dragged the mouse (**Figure 12.25**). Furthermore, that clip is trimmed to occupy only the duration of the gap.

Figure 12.24 Dragging the clip pins it to the video, noted by a small pin icon.

To un-pin a background audio clip:

1. Select the pinned clip.

2. Choose Un-Pin Music Track from the Edit menu or the contextual menu.

Before pinning

After pinning

Figure 12.25 When you pin a background clip (1) that has another clip following it (2), the later clip fills in the space vacated by the pinned clip.

✔ Tips

- If you un-pin the clip in Figure 12.25, it does not return to its former position, but now appears at the end of the background music. However, clip 2 in that example regains its full duration.

- Remember that you can use the Audio Adjustments tool to modify the volume and fades of background audio tracks.

- iMovie creates a 1-second crossfade between adjoining background audio clips.

Ducking slider

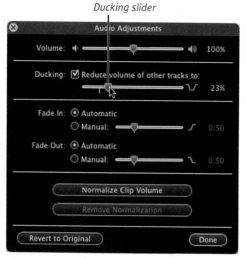

Figure 12.26 Ducking reduces the volume in other clips so you can feature the audio in the selected clip.

Ducking Audio

When you're working with multiple layers of sound, at some point there's just too much audio competing against itself. To draw attention to the audio of one clip, enable ducking, which reduces the volume of other audio for the duration of that clip. Ducking is often used to hear dialog: when someone starts talking, the background music fades back (but doesn't go silent).

To duck audio:

1. Click a video or audio clip to select it. Background audio clips cannot be ducked.

2. Click the Audio Adjustments button (or press the A key) to bring up the Audio Adjustments window.

3. Click the Ducking checkbox to enable the feature (**Figure 12.26**). The volume of surrounding clips is reduced to 15 percent of their volume setting.

4. Drag the Ducking slider to make the other clips louder (drag to the right) or softer (drag to the left).

5. Click Done to exit the window.

✔ Tip

■ iMovie automatically applies fades when ducking, so the surrounding audio smoothly drops down to the ducking level at the start of the clip and then goes back up to full volume at the end.

Trimming Audio Clips

As with video, you can trim audio clips to the duration that works best for your project. For quick adjustments, simply drag the edges in the Project Browser. For more precise edits, or to edit background music clips, open the clip in the trimmer.

To trim an audio clip in the Project Browser:

1. Position the mouse pointer at the left or right edge of the audio clip. The pointer becomes a double-ended arrow icon (**Figure 12.27**).

2. Click and drag to reveal or hide the audio (**Figure 12.28**).

To trim an audio clip in the trimmer:

1. Select an audio clip and choose Trim from the Edit menu, or press Command-R. For background music clips, you can also click the Clip Duration button in the upper-left corner of the clip.

   The trimmer appears in place of the Project Browser (**Figure 12.29**). The lighter-colored area indicates the audible portion of the clip.

2. Drag the yellow handles to set the start and end points of the clip. The waveforms will help you locate where dialog begins and ends, for example. As you drag, the Viewer displays the video frame beneath the playhead.

   If you're trimming a background audio clip that has been automatically shortened due to a pinned clip (see Figure 12.25, earlier), iMovie displays the audible portion of the waveforms in a light color and the inaudible portions in black (**Figure 12.30**). However, because the clip is being trimmed automatically by iMovie, the end point does not change.

Figure 12.27 The pointer's icon changes to indicate that you can trim the audio clip.

Figure 12.28 Drag to change the duration of the clip.

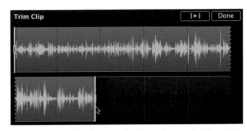

Figure 12.29 The trimmer displays the audio clip with waveforms to help you make more precise edits.

End of audible portion

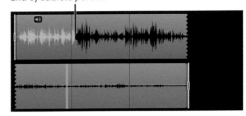

Figure 12.30 Trimming a background music clip.

TRIMMING AUDIO CLIPS

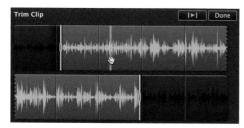

Figure 12.31 Drag the middle of the selection to slip the clip and retain the same duration.

3. To slip the clip (adjust the start and end points without changing the clip's duration), click the middle of the selection and drag (**Figure 12.31**).

4. Press the Play button to play back the clip (which also includes any other audio at the same location in the filmstrip) or click Done to exit the trimmer.

✔ Tip

■ You don't have to select an audio clip before you trim it. When you click and drag a clip's edge, it's automatically selected for you.

Adding Just the Audio from a Video Clip

Earlier versions of iMovie included a feature that let you extract the audio portion of a video clip. That command is gone in iMovie '08, but the feature is still there. You can use this technique when you want just the audio of a video clip.

For example, let's say your step-brother captured better audio of your sister's wedding on his camcorder, but your vantage point made for better visuals. You can silence your video clips and insert the audio from his.

To add audio from a video clip:

1. Select a video clip (or portion of a clip) in the Event Browser.

2. Hold the Command and Shift keys down and drag the clip to the point in the Project Browser's filmstrip at which you want the audio to appear (**Figure 12.32**). The audio from the video clip appears as a new audio clip pinned to the filmstrip (**Figure 12.33**).

✔ Tip

■ Extracting audio clips makes it possible to start playing audio before the visuals begin (or after they're done). For example, I wanted to transition from the title image to an opening shot of a waterfall (**Figure 12.34**). Using an imported black still image, I displayed a few seconds of black frames with just the sound of the waterfall, then faded in on the video of the waterfall. The audio and visuals weren't synchronized, but that didn't matter because the clip was an establishing shot with background sounds.

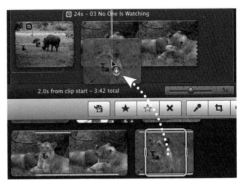

Figure 12.32 Hold Command-Shift while dragging a video clip to the Project Browser to add just the audio.

Figure 12.33 Instead of inserting the video at the play-head, the audio appears pinned to that spot.

Imported black still image   Waterfall clip audio

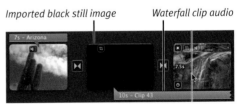

Figure 12.34 Extracting the audio from the third clip allowed me to begin playing the sound of the waterfall during a few seconds of black frames, then fade in on the visual of the waterfall itself (top). You can view this clip at www.jeffcarlson.com/imovievqs/.

TRANSITIONS AND TITLES

Transitions can be equally wonderful and terrible things. They can move you from one scene to another without the abruptness of a straightforward cut, or help define a movie's pace by easing you gently into or out of a scene.

But transitions can also become a distraction, because you're introducing motion or visuals that weren't recorded by the camera. Too many transitions can be like using too many fonts in a word processing application: pretty soon, all you see is the style, not the content.

Titles, however, are another story. In Hollywood, movie titles aren't mere words that flash up on the screen. Actors, agents, and studio executives negotiate for the length of time a person's name appears, how large or small the typeface is, whether the name comes before or after the movie title, and all sorts of other conditions that inflame my aversion to fine print. You won't deal with any of that, because the other aspects of movie titles—i.e., actually *creating* them— are made extraordinarily easy in iMovie.

As with a lot of iMovie capabilities, you're creating elements quickly and cheaply that used to cost a fortune for studios and filmmakers.

Adding Transitions

Adding a transition to your movie is as easy as dragging and dropping an icon. You can then edit the transition in place (and best of all, you don't have to wait for it to render as in the old days of iMovie).

To add a transition:

1. Click the Transitions button in the toolbar, choose Transitions from the Window menu, or press Command-4. The Transitions Browser appears to the right of the Event Browser (**Figure 13.1**).

2. Choose a transition from the browser. The icons play a preview of the effect when you move your pointer over them.

3. Drag the transition to the intersection of two clips in the Project Browser (**Figure 13.2**). (Transitions can be added to the beginning and end of the movie as well.) A transition icon appears (**Figure 13.3**).

To delete a transition:

1. Select the transition in the Project Browser.

2. Press the Delete key, or choose Cut or Clear from the Edit menu. The sections of clips that were used by the transition are restored.

✔ Tips

■ Leave enough padding in your clips to accommodate transitions. Otherwise, your transitions won't display correctly.

■ Each transition type has its own icon in the Project Browser, making it easy to see at a glance which style is applied.

■ To change a transition in your movie to a different transition style, simply drag the new one over the top of the existing one.

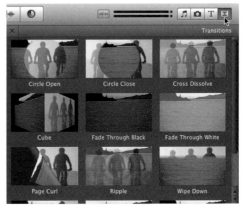

Figure 13.1 Choose from a variety of transition effects in the Transitions Browser.

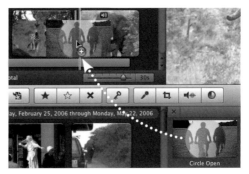

Figure 13.2 Drag a transition icon between two clips to add it.

Transition icon

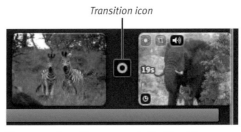

Figure 13.3 Transitions appear in the filmstrip as small icons between clips.

Figure 13.4 Change a transition's duration in this dialog instead of dragging endpoints in the browser.

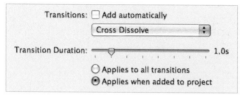

Figure 13.5 The Transition Duration slider applies to all transitions in the project or ones next added.

To change a transition's duration:

1. Select a transition in the movie.

2. Control-click to bring up the contextual menu and choose Set Duration; you can also choose Set Duration from the Edit menu or press Command-R.

3. In the dialog that appears, enter a new time in the Duration field (**Figure 13.4**).

4. Click the radio button corresponding to how widely the setting is to be applied: to just the selected clip or to all transitions in the project.

To change the default duration of transitions:

1. If you prefer that all new transitions be longer than the default half second amount, choose Project Properties from the File menu or the contextual menu, or press Command-J.

2. In the Project Properties dialog that appears, set a new time using the Transition Duration slider (**Figure 13.5**).

3. Choose how the setting will be applied: to all transitions in the project or to transitions added from that point forward.

4. Click OK to apply the settings. If you chose Applies to all transitions, the durations of existing transitions are changed.

✔ Tip

■ You can move a transition to another spot in the filmstrip by dragging it to the new location. Hold Option as you drag to create a copy of the transition—it doesn't copy any of the footage, but applies its style and duration to the new clips that surround it.

To automatically add transitions:

1. Choose Project Properties from the File menu or press Command-J.

2. Mark the Add automatically checkbox.

3. Choose a transition style from the popup menu (**Figure 13.6**).

4. Set a length for the transitions in the Transition Duration slider.

5. Click OK. In the new dialog that appears, choose one option (**Figure 13.7**):

   ▲ **Overlap ends and shorten clip.** iMovie uses the visible footage to generate the transition, resulting in a shorter clip (see the sidebar opposite).

   ▲ **Extend ends and keep duration the same (where possible).** iMovie uses excess footage that's outside the trim points to build the transition.

6. Click OK to apply the transitions throughout the project. When automatic transitions are enabled, you can't delete them manually.

To turn off automatic transitions:

1. Choose Project Properties from the File menu or press Command-J.

2. Disable the Add automatically checkbox.

3. In the dialog that appears, choose how iMovie handles the footage that the transitions were using (**Figure 13.8**).

   If you choose Leave transitions in current locations, you can selectively delete the ones you no longer want to keep.

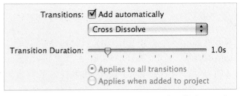

Figure 13.6 If you prefer to let iMovie do all the work, set it to add transitions automatically in the project.

Figure 13.7 iMovie offers two methods of building the frames that make up each transition.

Figure 13.8 Turning off automatic transitions.

Most Valuable Transitions

In most situations, you'll find yourself using only a couple of transitions: Cross Dissolve and Fade Through Black. I'm also partial to Fade Through White, in the right context. The others, to me, are usually too flashy for regular use.

The Fade Through Black transition does double duty: Putting it at the beginning of the movie gives you a fade-in; at the end, you get a fade-out. You're essentially transitioning from nothing (black) to the first clip and vice-versa for the last clip.

ADDING TRANSITIONS

iMovie's Habit of Stealing Time

As you add transitions, you may notice something odd happening: your movie is getting *shorter*. Is it possible to add things to a movie and still end up with less than when you started? (And if so, does it apply to eating ice cream?)

Yes. (But no to the ice cream.) Here's how iMovie steals time using transitions (**Figure 13.9**):

1. For the sake of not straining my math abilities, let's assume we want to add a Cross Dissolve transition between two 10-second clips. In order to maintain a comfortable pace, we decide to make our transition 2 seconds long.

2. We drag the transition into place between the clips, and notice that each clip has become 8 seconds in length, not 9 seconds (to split a 2-second transition between two clips leaves 1 second for each clip: $10 - 1 = 9$).

3. The mystery is solved when we look at how iMovie is building the transition. It needs to start dissolving one clip into the other clip at the very beginning of the transition, so iMovie merges 2 seconds of each clip, removing 4 seconds total. The transition is still 2 seconds in duration, but required 4 seconds to perform the blends. Think of it as tightening a belt: you still have the same amount of material, but the overlap where the buckle rests allows you to encompass a smaller area.

Total movie time before transition: 20 seconds

Clips before adding transition

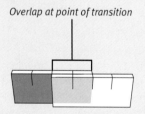

Total movie time decreased to 18 seconds after adding transition

Two-second transition steals a total of four seconds from the affected clips.

Overlap at point of transition

Figure 13.9 Some transitions, such as Cross Dissolve, need to overlap two clips in order to merge the number of frames needed for the effect. This creates a shorter overall movie.

Adding Titles

In ages past, the way to add a title to a movie was to laboriously set it up in the camera, scrolling through each letter (depending on the camera model) to have the date or a scene name burned to tape forever. Long before that, of course, editors shot footage of title cards that provided the "dialog" in silent movies. Thankfully, we've come a long way since then.

To add a title:

1. Click the Titles button in the toolbar, choose Titles from the Window menu, or press Command-3. The Titles Browser appears to the right of the Event Browser (**Figure 13.10**).

2. Choose a title style from the browser.

3. Drag the title's icon onto a clip in the Project Browser (**Figure 13.11**). The blue highlighted area indicates where the title will be applied: a partial highlight indicates the beginning or end of the clip; if the entire clip is highlighted, the title will match the duration of the clip.

   The title appears as a blue clip above the video clip (**Figure 13.12**).

To display a title against a black background:

◆ Drag a title to the space between two clips. When you release the mouse button, a new blank clip pushes aside the clip that follows the title and displays the text on a black background, rather than overlaying it on clip footage (**Figure 13.13**).

To reposition a title:

◆ Click within the title clip and drag it to a new position on the filmstrip.

Figure 13.10 Who are these people? Well, ignore them and pay attention to each thumbnail's title style.

Title will occupy the first portion of the video clip.

Figure 13.11 The blue highlight indicates the duration of the title when you release the mouse button.

Title clip

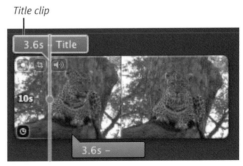

Figure 13.12 Titles appear as blue clips anchored above the video.

New black clip —

Figure 13.13 Dropping a title in front of a clip superimposes the text over a new black clip.

Figure 13.14 A title can span multiple clips. Simply drag the left or right edges to change its duration.

Figure 13.15 The Title Fade Duration setting applies to all titles in the project.

To change a title's duration:

◆ Drag the left or right edge of the title clip (**Figure 13.14**).

To set a title's fade duration:

1. Choose Project Properties from the File menu or press Command-J.

2. Choose a new value, up to 2 seconds, using the Title Fade Duration slider (**Figure 13.15**). iMovie fades-in the start of the title and fades-out the end over the time you specify. Click OK.

To delete a title:

1. Select the offending title clip.

2. Press the Delete key. You can also choose Cut or Clear from the Edit menu.

✔ Tips

■ Remember that not everyone may be able to read as fast as you. Give your viewers plenty of time to read your title—without boring them, of course.

■ Remember at the end of the last chapter where I played audio of a waterfall over a black clip before the waterfall visuals appeared? In that case I imported a still image that was solid black, but you can also use this title trick to add black frames without importing anything. Drag a title from the Titles Browser to the space before a clip to create the black clip. Then simply delete the title clip above it. You can then change the duration of the black clip as if it were a regular image.

ADDING TITLES

143

Editing Title Text

iMovie may not offer many title styles, but it does give you quite a bit of control over the text's appearance.

To edit title text:

1. Click a title in the Project Browser to select it. The Viewer becomes editable (**Figure 13.16**).

2. Click within the text to position your pointer and select the text you want to change (**Figure 13.17**).

3. Type new title text. Feel free to click the Play button to see how the text appears above the footage.

4. When you're finished editing the text (including any formatting, described just ahead), click Done.

To insert special characters:

1. Click within the text field to position the pointer.

2. Choose Special Characters from the Edit menu, or press Command-Option-T.

3. Select a character from the Characters Palette.

4. Click the Insert button. The character appears in the text field (**Figure 13.18**).

✔ Tip

■ When entering text for the Scrolling Credits title, you can include more than just the four placeholders provided. To get the text to line up properly, press the Tab key to insert a tab character before and after the name in the left column.

Figure 13.16 Selecting a title turns the Viewer into a text-editing environment.

Figure 13.17 The title can be edited much as if you were working in a text editor or word processor.

Figure 13.18 Take advantage of the Characters palette to locate symbols and "dingbats."

Figure 13.19 The Fonts palette is a system-wide control for formatting text.

Text Color button

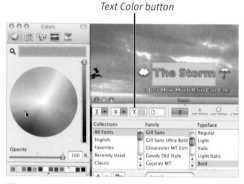

Figure 13.20 Select a text color from the Colors palette.

Background color block

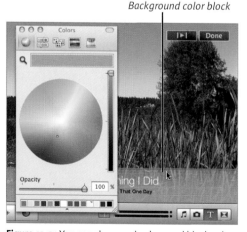

Figure 13.21 You can change a background block color.

Editing Text Style

Now that you've entered some text, it's time to give it style: select a color and a typeface, and change the type size.

To edit text style:

1. Click a title in the Project Browser if it's not already selected.

2. Select the text to edit.

3. Click the Show Fonts button to bring up the Fonts palette (**Figure 13.19**).

To change text color:

1. In the Fonts palette, click the Text Color button. The Colors palette appears (**Figure 13.20**).

2. Click within the color wheel to select a color, or click one of the buttons at the top to change selectors (such as sliders or even Crayon colors). You can try as many colors as you like while the palette is visible, and see them applied to text in the Viewer.

3. Click the close button in the upper-left corner of the Colors palette to accept the last color you applied.

To change background text block color:

1. After adding a title containing a background text block, such as Transparent – White, click the block to select it. The Colors palette automatically appears (**Figure 13.21**).

2. Click within the Colors palette to select a color.

3. Close the Colors palette or click elsewhere to deselect the background block.

To specify font and size:

1. In the Fonts palette, choose a font and style from the Family and Typeface columns (**Figure 13.22**).

2. Drag the Size slider to increase or decrease the type size.

✔ Tips

■ To ensure that fonts appear smooth in titles, use Adobe PostScript, TrueType, or OpenType fonts. These include the fonts that ship with Mac OS X.

■ The array of typographic controls in the Fonts palette is almost bewildering. In addition to fonts and sizes, you can specify text alignment, line spacing, kerning (the amount of space between letters), and even fine-tune the drop shadow. The whole set of controls are fun to play with.

Figure 13.22 The typographic possibilities are extensive using the Fonts palette.

Part 3
Sharing from iMovie

SCORING YOUR MOVIE IN GARAGEBAND

14

A movie's soundtrack doesn't need to consist of popular music—in fact, most films are scored instrumentally, according to the needs of each scene. If you have musical leanings, you may want to do your own scoring. With the inclusion of GarageBand in Apple's iLife suite, you can (even if you're not particularly musical, like me).

With a musical instrument and some hardware to get the audio into your Mac, you can perform your own music. Personally, I like GarageBand because I can choose from hundreds of existing background loops and create segments that are just as long as I need them to be. Those loops are also copyright- and royalty-free, so I don't need to worry about securing rights if I decide to release the movie in public.

Sharing to GarageBand

Send your entire movie to GarageBand, where you can build music with the video as reference. This option is great for timing music cues with your movie.

To share your movie to GarageBand:

1. Choose Media Browser from the Share menu, or Control-click the project name and choose Share to Media Browser from the contextual menu.

2. Click the checkbox for the size that matches the final output of your movie (**Figure 14.1**).

3. Click the Publish button. iMovie compresses the movie and prepares it for use by the other iLife applications.

4. Launch GarageBand.

5. Choose Show Media Browser from the Control menu. The browser appears at the right edge of the window.

6. Click the Movies button and expand the iMovie item to view your projects in the list (**Figure 14.2**). (If you didn't share the movie in Step 1, GarageBand won't display a preview.)

7. Drag the shared movie to the Timeline to add it to the project. It appears on a new video track (**Figure 14.3**).

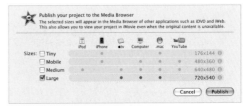

Figure 14.1 Share your movie to GarageBand to start the scoring process.

Figure 14.2 The movie you shared in iMovie is available in GarageBand's Media Browser.

Video Track   *Movie thumbnails*   *Video preview*

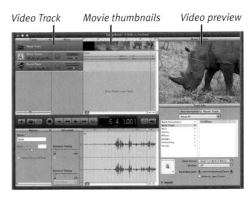

Figure 14.3 GarageBand includes your shared movie as reference to help determine timing of the music.

Mute Track button

Figure 14.4 Make the Video Sound track silent so you can focus on building the score in other tracks.

✔ Tips

- If you plan on bringing the score back into iMovie for further editing (described later in this chapter), share the movie using the Mobile version; the audio settings are the same as Medium and Large, but you don't have the overhead in time and disk space required by the full-quality version.

- All audio from your movie appears on one track in GarageBand, even if you had multiple tracks set up in iMovie. You may want to mute the Movie Sound track while working on your score (**Figure 14.4**).

- Having your video appear within Garage-Band is an enormous help, but it comes at a cost: even on fast machines, playback can be stuttery. GarageBand is simply a resource hog. You can regain some performance by locking audio tracks (click the padlock icon below the track name); this tells GarageBand to create a temporary "mixdown" of the locked tracks, which requires less processing power.

- I'm just scratching the surface of Garage-Band in these few pages. Be sure to read the program's online help, or pick up a good book (such as Jeff Tolbert's *Take Control of GarageBand* titles, www. takecontrolbooks.com).

Making Music Using GarageBand

With a MIDI keyboard or guitar and amp you can start recording your own tunes. For simplicity's sake, however, I'm going to concentrate on using GarageBand's built-in loops to create a song.

To create a music loop in GarageBand:

1. Display the Loop Browser by clicking the Loop Browser button, choosing Show Loop Browser from the Control menu, or pressing Command-L (**Figure 14.5**).

2. From the first three columns of the Loop Browser, click an instrument name. You can also choose multiple musical styles (from the next three columns) to refine the list of loops. The list of available loops matching your selections appears in the right-hand column (**Figure 14.6**).

3. Click a loop to hear it. The loop will continue to play until you click it again or click another loop.

4. Choose a loop and drag it to Garage-Band's Timeline to add it to your song (**Figure 14.7**).

5. Press the Play button or the spacebar to preview your song. I recommend also clicking the Cycle button (which has a picture of circled arrows) so that the song repeats as you're working. You can always hit spacebar again to stop playback.

6. The Time display shows measures, beats, and ticks. Click the small LCD mode icon in the left corner of the display to switch to Time (hours, minutes, seconds, fractions) (**Figure 14.8**).

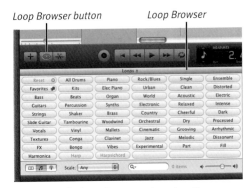

Loop Browser button   Loop Browser

Figure 14.5 The Loop Browser categorizes Garage-Band's loops according to instrument and genre.

Loop list

Figure 14.6 As you make instrument selections, the loop list displays loops that match your criteria.

Figure 14.7 Drag a loop from the Loop Browser to GarageBand's Timeline to create a new track.

LCD mode button

Figure 14.8 I'm much more familiar with absolute time than with measures, beats, and ticks. Changing the Time display helps to define the song's length.

Region (selected)   *Loop pointer*

Figure 14.9 The region is the track's audio clip. Drag the edge of the region with the loop pointer to extend the duration of the loop.

Rounded corners indicate a loop within a region.

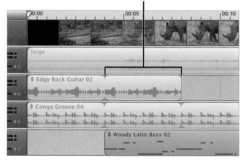

Figure 14.10 Loops are created so that they play cleanly from start to finish without breaks.

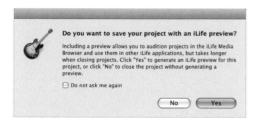

Figure 14.11 If you don't save your GarageBand project with an iLife preview, you won't be able to import the song into iMovie later.

7. Position your mouse pointer at the right edge of the loop you added, which GarageBand calls a *region*, so that the cursor changes to a rounded circle, called the *loop pointer* (**Figure 14.9**).

8. Drag the loop pointer to the right to extend the region for as long as you want it to continue playing within your song. Rounded-corner breaks within the region indicate where the loop starts and ends (**Figure 14.10**).

9. Repeat steps 2 through 4 to select another loop and add it to the Timeline as a new track. Add as many combinations as you like (guitar, drums, etc.) until the song sounds good to you.

✔ Tips

■ If the GarageBand window is too narrow, the Loop Browser and Video Preview won't appear at the same time. Extend the width of the window to see both.

■ You don't need to create a brand new track for each loop you add—they can coexist in the same tracks. But separating out the tracks makes it easier to edit.

■ When you close the project, GarageBand asks if you want to save an iLife preview (**Figure 14.11**). If you click Yes, iMovie will be able to import the song from the Media pane.

MAKING MUSIC USING GARAGEBAND

Getting the Score Back into iMovie

When you share your movie to GarageBand, iMovie assumes that you've finished editing and are ready to hand it off. But what if you want to go back and do more editing? There's no round-trip method to automatically pass the soundtrack back to iMovie. However, it is possible to import the song manually.

To import your song into iMovie:

1. In GarageBand, mute the Movie Sound track (because it's already present in your iMovie project) and close the project.

2. In iMovie, bring up the Music and Sound Effects Browser.

3. From the audio list, choose GarageBand to display a list of your GarageBand files.

4. Drag the song you created to the Project Browser to add the song as a background music clip (**Figure 14.12**). Only songs saved with an iLife preview (indicated by a guitar icon) can be added in this way.

5. iMovie warns you that the published project has been modified (**Figure 14.13**); click OK.

✔ Tips

- If you change the song in GarageBand, it won't automatically be updated in iMovie. You'll need to import the Garage-Band file again.

- You may need to quit and restart iMovie for it to recognize new GarageBand songs you've created.

Figure 14.12 When you import a GarageBand song, even if it includes video footage in GarageBand, iMovie brings in only the audio.

Figure 14.13 iMovie keeps track of which version of your movie was shared; if you change it, iMovie alerts you to avoid accidental editing.

GETTING THE SCORE BACK INTO iMOVIE

Sharing to iTunes and Online

15

You may be creating movies that will live only on your hard disk, for your eyes only, never to be seen by anyone. More likely, though, your movies are meant to be viewed. You can export the movie to a DVD and mail it to your relatives—if you don't mind purchasing the media, filling it with movies (or just using a few minutes of it for one movie), then paying to mail it across the country or around the world. Where's the instant gratification in that?

Instead (or in addition), send your movie to the grandparents by email or post it to the Web directly.

Yet another option is to transfer the movie to an iPod, iPhone, or handheld organizer. You can now show off your entire film library to your friends over lunch or coffee.

Sharing to iTunes

If you own an iPod, iPhone, or an Apple TV, the only way to get media onto it is through iTunes. iMovie can format your movies properly for those devices and ensure that you'll be able to watch your movies almost anywhere.

To share a project to iTunes:

1. With the project selected in the Project List, choose iTunes from the Share menu.

2. Mark one or more checkboxes for each size of movie you want to generate (**Figure 15.1**).

3. Click the Publish button. iMovie encodes the movie for the sizes you specified (**Figure 15.2**). When finished, it adds the movie to iTunes (**Figure 15.3**).

   You can then watch the movie in iTunes or synchronize your device and watch it there.

   iMovie displays an icon in the Project List that indicates which sizes have been published, as well as a small banner in the Project Browser with the destination (**Figure 15.4**). Click the banner to switch to iTunes and view the movie there.

To remove a project from iTunes:

◆ With the project selected in the Project List, choose Remove from iTunes from the Share menu. The movie no longer appears in iTunes.

✔ Tip

■ Position the mouse pointer over the "i" icon to the right of each size to view a summary of that size's compression settings and an estimate of how much space the resulting file will be on disk.

Figure 15.1 iMovie indicates which sizes will work on which Apple (surprise!) devices.

Figure 15.2 Take a break while iMovie encodes the movie into the formats you chose.

Figure 15.3 The encoded movie appears in the Movies list in iTunes.

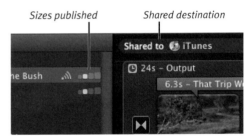

Figure 15.4 You can tell at a glance where the movie has been published.

SHARING TO iTUNES

Figure 15.5 More devices are represented when you share with the Media Browser.

Figure 15.6 After sharing with the Media Browser, the movie appears in Keynote's Media palette.

Sharing with the Media Browser

We touched on this briefly in the last chapter, but another way to share your movie is to make it available to the Media Browser, a resource used by the iLife applications, as well as the iWork suite. The benefit of the Media Browser is that you don't have to export a file and keep track of it; supported applications know where to look.

To share with the Media Browser:

1. With a project selected in the Project List, choose Media Browser from the Share menu. You can also Control-click a project and choose Share with Media Browser from the contextual menu.

2. Mark one or more checkboxes for each size of movie you want to generate (**Figure 15.5**).

3. Click the Publish button. iMovie encodes the movie for the sizes you specified. When finished, the movie is available to other applications (**Figure 15.6**).

✔ Tip

■ The Large size maxes out at 960 by 540 pixels, even if you're working on 1080i video.

Publishing to YouTube

YouTube has emerged as a popular free destination for uploading video files and sharing them easily. iMovie lets you upload directly to YouTube, bypassing a number of hoops you'd otherwise have to jump through. You'll need a free YouTube account

To share a movie to YouTube:

1. With the project selected in the Project List, choose YouTube from the Share menu or Control-click the project and choose Publish to YouTube from the contextual menu.

2. In the dialog that appears, click the Add button to sign into your account (**Figure 15.7**). (If you don't yet have an account, you're given the opportunity to sign up.)

3. You're taken to a Web page that asks you to give iMovie permission to write content to your site. Click the Allow button, then return to iMovie and confirm the sign-in.

4. Choose a category; enter a title; and optionally write up a description of your movie. To make your movie easy for others to find, enter keywords into the Tags field.

5. Choose a size to publish—either Mobile or Medium.

6. To restrict who can view the movie, click the option marked Make this movie private.

7. Click Next to review the YouTube Terms of Service, and then click the Publish button. After encoding and uploading the video, iMovie points you to its location on the Web (**Figure 15.8**).

   In iMovie, a banner above the movie notes that the movie has been published to YouTube, with options to tell a friend or visit the page (**Figure 15.9**).

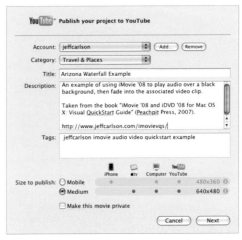

Figure 15.7 Enter all the information about a movie here and you won't have to do it on the Web later.

Figure 15.8 Once published, your video is available to the world.

Figure 15.9 If you forget the location of your movie, go back to iMovie and click the Visit button in the YouTube banner.

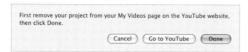

Figure 15.10 Removing a video from YouTube requires that you first manually delete the movie from YouTube.

Figure 15.11 Click Remove Video to purge the movie from YouTube's servers.

To remove a movie from YouTube:

1. Select the project in the Project List and choose Remove from YouTube from the Share menu.

2. In the dialog that appears, click the Go to YouTube button (**Figure 15.10**).

3. On your My Videos page, locate the movie and click the Remove Video button (**Figure 15.11**).

4. Go back to iMovie and click the Done button. The YouTube banner is removed.

Publishing to a .Mac Web Gallery

If you subscribe to Apple's .Mac service, you can take advantage of its Web Gallery that gives you a presence on the Web with a minimum of fuss.

To publish to a .Mac Web Gallery:

1. With the project selected in the Project List, choose .Mac Web Gallery from the Share menu or Control-click the project and choose the same item from the contextual menu.

2. In the dialog that appears, enter a title and description (**Figure 15.12**).

3. Select the sizes you want to upload. You can select as many as you'd like; your site's visitors can choose which size they want to view based on their Internet service.

4. To let people save the movie file to their hard disks, enable the option to Allow movies to be downloaded.

5. Click the Show project on Web Gallery home page box to make the movie accessible to someone who visits the main page of your Web Gallery.

6. Click Publish. iMovie encodes and uploads the movie(s). When it's finished, you can send an email announcement or visit the site directly (**Figure 15.13**). iMovie also adds a new banner to the project (**Figure 15.14**).

To remove a movie from the Web Gallery:

1. With the project selected, choose Remove from .Mac from the Share menu.

2. In the confirmation dialog that appears, click OK. The movie is removed from the gallery.

Figure 15.12 Set the options here for publishing a movie to your .Mac Web Gallery.

Figure 15.13 Visitors can view and download your movies from your .Mac Web Gallery.

Figure 15.14 iMovie notes where a project has been published above the filmstrip.

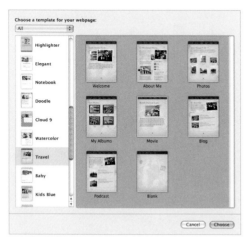

Figure 15.15 iWeb offers lots of ready-made Web templates.

Figure 15.16 Drag the shared movie from the Media palette to the placeholder iWeb created.

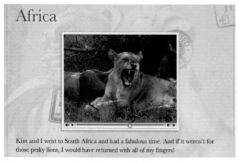

Figure 15.17 Replace the sample text with your own clever musings and witty anecdotes.

Publishing to the Web Using iWeb

For more control over how the movie is presented on the Web, you can use iWeb to publish it to your Web site. iWeb uses the Media Browser to grab content from other iLife applications.

To publish to the Web using iWeb:

1. Share your movie to the Media Browser as described earlier in this chapter.

2. In iWeb, choose a theme from the column at the left (**Figure 15.15**).

3. Click the Choose button. iWeb creates a new page.

4. Click the Media button to bring up the Media palette.

5. Click the Movies button in the Media palette and locate your movie.

6. Drag the icon for your movie to the placeholder on the iWeb page (**Figure 15.16**).

7. Type the page title, movie title, and page description text in the fields provided (**Figure 15.17**).

8. Click the Publish button to create and upload the new page to your site.

To make changes to your page:

1. In iWeb, load the page by clicking its page icon in the left column.

2. Make any changes you want on the page. The page icon turns red to indicate that it's been edited but not published.

3. Click the Publish button.

Writing HTML

iWeb makes it extremely easy to publish movies to the Web, but you may already have a site set up, you aren't a .Mac member, or you just like to dig into the code out of pure textual geeky joy.

This, of course, isn't a book about HTML, so I'm going to assume that you know the basics about coding Web pages, and that you have an application (such as Bare Bones Software's BBEdit, or even TextEdit) that you use to build pages. If that's not the case, check out Elizabeth Castro's book *HTML for the World Wide Web with XHTML and CSS: Visual QuickStart Guide*, which remains the best HTML guide I've read.

That said, there are two ways of going about it: You can copy the file to your Web directory (provided by your Internet service provider) then link directly to it; or you can embed the movie on a Web page so that it's part of the page's layout.

To link to a QuickTime movie file:

1. In your HTML editing application, enter the following code where you want your movie link to appear. The user will see only the linked text; clicking it will download the movie.

   ```
   <a href="http://www.youraddress.com/
   sample.mov">Click here</a>
   ```

2. Insert the real names of your Web address and movie filename in place of *youraddress.com* and *sample.mov* (**Figure 15.18**). For example, a movie on my Web site would look like this (go ahead and put the URL below into your Web browser to view the movie).

   ```
   <a href="http://www.necoffee.com/
   imovievqs/secretmovie.mov">Is it
   really a secret?</a>
   ```

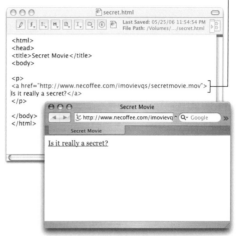

HTML text that creates link

Figure 15.18 Add a simple Web link that points to your QuickTime movie file. The HTML text in the top window creates the Web page in the bottom window.

Deciphering HTML Attributes

So what is all that junk I threw in there? Here's a breakdown of the tag attributes:

OBJECT CLASSID: To work properly under Windows, a QuickTime movie must be defined as an object. The CLASSID value identifies the content as a Quick-Time movie.

WIDTH and **HEIGHT**: These values tell the browser the width and height of your movie in pixels.

CODEBASE: This URL gives Internet Explorer for Windows some necessary information about the QuickTime format.

PARAM: This is a parameter of the object, which consists of a name and a value. SRC is the URL that points to your movie file; AUTOPLAY tells the browser whether to automatically play the movie when it loads (in this case "true" means yes); CONTROLLER tells the browser whether to display the QuickTime controller beneath the movie (in this case "false" means no).

EMBED: This is the tag that actually puts your QuickTime movie on the page. It includes the same attributes as PARAM, though in a slightly more compact fashion. A Web page that contains only this tag will display the movie correctly in all Web browsers except Internet Explorer 5.5 and later for Windows.

PLUGINSPAGE: This tells the browser where to go in the event that the Quick-Time plug-in is not installed.

</EMBED> and **</OBJECT>**: These are closing tags, indicating the end of the commands.

To embed the movie on a page:

◆ In your HTML editing application, enter the following code where you want the movie to appear. Be sure to change the two instances of `sample.mov` to your actual filename, plus the two instances where the width and height are defined.

```
<OBJECT CLASSID="clsid:02BF25D5-8C17-4B23-BC80-D3488ABDDC6B" WIDTH="160" HEIGHT="144" CODEBASE="http://www.apple.com/qtactivex/qtplugin.cab">
<PARAM name="SRC" VALUE="sample.mov">
<PARAM name="AUTOPLAY" VALUE="true">
<PARAM name="CONTROLLER" VALUE="false">
<EMBED SRC="sample.mov" WIDTH="160" HEIGHT="144" AUTOPLAY="true" CONTROLLER="false" PLUGINSPAGE="http://www.apple.com/quicktime/download/">
</EMBED>
</OBJECT>
```

Note that the unintelligible gobbledy-gook following `CLASSID=` must be entered exactly as shown; it's required for viewing the page properly in Microsoft Internet Explorer 5.5 and later under Windows.

WRITING HTML

Creating a Poster Movie

Accessing a QuickTime movie on the Web introduces one big problem: whether you link to it directly or embed it onto a page, the entire movie begins downloading. Depending on the size of the movie, this could slow your browser or other Internet applications while the movie is being fetched.

As an alternative, create a poster movie, which displays a one-frame movie that your visitors can click to initiate the download. (Sometimes this can be frustrating: I've clicked on links expecting the movie to load in the background while I'm working on something else, only to realize that I needed to then click the poster movie to get the download started. At least this route gives the visitor the option to start the movie at her convenience.) The poster movie has the added benefit of preloading the QuickTime plug-in before the movie starts.

Creating a poster movie involves two steps: creating the one-frame movie using Quick-Time Player (the Pro version), then adjusting the EMBED tag in the HTML to handle it properly.

To create the poster movie:

1. Open your movie in QuickTime Player.

2. Use the movie control buttons or the location indicator to find a frame you'd like to use as the poster movie's image (**Figure 15.19**).

3. Choose Copy from the Edit menu, or press Command-C. This copies the selected frame.

4. Create a new movie by choosing New (Command-N) from the File menu.

5. Choose Paste (Command-V) from the Edit menu. Your copied frame appears as its own one-frame movie.

Figure 15.19 Use the Playhead in QuickTime Player to locate the frame you'd like to use for the poster movie.

Figure 15.20 To make the poster movie work, your one frame needs to be saved as a QuickTime movie, not as an individual image format like TIFF or JPEG.

Figure 15.21 The end result is a single image that shows up in place of the movie, but one you can click to immediately begin playing the movie.

6. Save the movie with a distinctive name, such as "Africa_CD-ROM_poster.mov", to use my example (**Figure 15.20**).

To embed the poster movie:

1. In your HTML editor, type the code you used to embed the movie (shown two pages back).

2. In the EMBED tag, add the HREF and TARGET attributes (underlined):

```
<EMBED SRC="sample_poster.
mov" WIDTH="160" HEIGHT="144"
AUTOPLAY="true"
CONTROLLER="false" HREF="sample.mov"
TARGET="myself" PLUGINSPAGE=
"http://www.apple.com/quicktime/
download/">
```

The EMBED tag tells the browser to first load the poster movie; the HREF tag tells it to load the real movie when clicked; and the TARGET tag instructs it to play the real movie in the same space as the poster movie.

3. Save and upload your files. When you view them in a Web browser, the poster image shows up first (**Figure 15.21**).

✔ Tips

■ If you're seeing only half of the movie controller, add 15 to the height values in the OBJECT and EMBED tags.

■ Be sure the controller attributes are set to "false," or else you'll see a controller in the poster movie, which can be confusing. Viewers might click the controller to play the movie, which works—but only plays the one frame.

■ It's a good idea to include instructions near the poster movie that say something like, "Click to play movie."

CREATING A POSTER MOVIE

EXPORTING MOVIES

Publishing your movies online isn't the only method of sharing them. iMovie can export them to various formats on your hard disk for use in other applications, or to give you more control over the movies' quality. It does this through Apple's QuickTime technology.

On the surface, QuickTime is a great little utility for playing movies on your Mac. I often visit www.apple.com/trailers/ to see which new movie trailer is ready for download—I click a link, and in a couple of minutes the clip is playing. (It's amazing what you can learn about filmmaking from trailers, by the way; they're some of the best sources for how to present ideas and images in a short time span.) Sometimes the movie appears in a window in your Web browser, while other times the QuickTime Player plays the movie.

Exporting the Movie

The Export command lets you export a file in one of iMovie's common video sizes to the location of your choosing on disk (versus copying it to the iTunes library, for example).

To export as a QuickTime movie:

1. With the project selected in the Project List, choose Export Movie from the Share menu, or press Command-E.

2. In the dialog that appears, navigate to the location on your hard disk (**Figure 16.1**).

3. Select a size to export by clicking its radio button. (The dimensions of the sizes vary depending on whether you're exporting DV or high-definition footage.)

4. Click the Export button to create the movie.

✔ Tip

■ iMovie offers a handy estimate of how much space the exported movie will occupy on disk (**Figure 16.2**).

Figure 16.1 Choose a destination and size to export the movie to disk.

Figure 16.2 Move the mouse pointer over the "i" icon to view an estimate of the project's size when saved.

Figure 16.3 Click the Options button in the Save dialog to access specific custom settings.

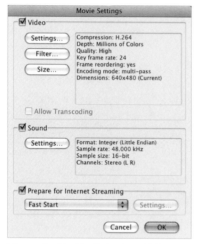

Figure 16.4 The Movie Settings dialog presents an overview of the current export settings.

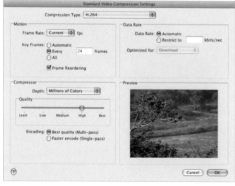

Figure 16.5 After that long progression of dialogs, you finally reach Compression Settings, where you can adjust the type and amount of compression used for exporting.

Exporting to QuickTime

iMovie's stock export settings are good for most situations, but you can also use other compression formats and options by way of QuickTime's Expert Settings.

To change image settings:

1. Select your project in the Project List.

2. Choose Export using QuickTime from the Share menu.

3. In the Save Exported File As dialog, make sure Movie to QuickTime Movie is selected in the Export popup menu, and click the Options button (**Figure 16.3**).

4. The Movie Settings dialog displays the current video and sound settings (**Figure 16.4**). To fine-tune the type and amount of video compression applied, click the Settings button under Video.

5. In the top area of the Compression Settings dialog, choose a compression method from the first popup menu (**Figure 16.5**). (Note that this dialog may look different depending on the compression type you're using. The option shown here is H.264.)

6. Move the Quality slider to the lowest level you can that maintains good image quality; the thumbnail shows you how much compression is being applied.

7. In the Motion area, select the number of frames per second from the Frame Rate popup menu.

continues on next page

EXPORTING TO QUICKTIME

8. Enter a number in the Key Frames Every [number] frames field to set how often a key frame is generated. Compression works by removing areas of a frame that have not changed since the preceding frame; to create a key frame, iMovie draws an entirely new frame.

9. To target a specific data rate, enter a value in the field labeled Restrict to [number] kbits/sec.

10. Click OK to return to Movie Settings.

11. Click OK to get back to the Save dialog, and then click the Save button to create the file.

✔ Tips

- The Sorenson Video codecs are highly regarded for having high video quality with good compression.

- The H.264 codec is mighty impressive, but it's also a resource hog, especially if you opt to use Multi-pass compression. It may take a while to export the file.

- If you want to export only the audio portion of your movie, choose Sound to AIFF from the Export popup menu in the Save Exported File As dialog. Or, when you're in the Movie Settings dialog, deselect the Video checkbox before exporting.

QuickTime versus QuickTime Pro

Every Mac comes with QuickTime, including the free QuickTime Player, which allows you to play back QuickTime movies and a host of other file formats (ranging from MPEG-formatted movies to MP3 audio files). If you're serious about optimizing your QuickTime movies for the Web, however, consider paying the $30 for a QuickTime Pro license, which turns QuickTime Player into a sophisticated movie editor. Not only does it give you an easy way to resize or recompress QuickTime movies, it also lets you save your movies into other formats, such as AVI, which Windows users can view if they don't have QuickTime installed.

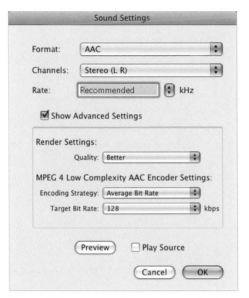

Figure 16.6 Choose an audio compressor to fine-tune how your movie's audio sounds after exporting.

To change audio settings:

1. Share your movie as described in the previous steps.

2. In the Sound portion of the Movie Settings dialog, click the Settings button to display sound-specific settings (**Figure 16.6**).

3. Choose a format from the Format popup menu. Some compressors include further settings, which are accessed by clicking the Show Advanced Settings checkbox. These usually determine how the data is encoded, or specify a data rate (or bit rate).

4. Decide whether the audio will play back in stereo or mono by choosing an option from the Channels popup menu. Stereo sounds better, but Mono offers a smaller file size.

5. In the Rate field, type a kHz value or select one from the popup menu to the right. Lower kHz settings will degrade the sound quality.

6. Click OK to exit the sound settings portion of the dialog.

✔ Tip

■ See **Table 16.1** on the next page for a summary of the video compressors included with QuickTime.

Video Compression Terms You Should Know

Codec: Short for compression/decompression; another name for a compressor.

Compression: The method used to reduce the size of the movie file while still retaining image quality. Video and audio compression make for a tricky business: you have to weigh the benefits of smaller file sizes (and therefore potentially faster downloads) against the desire to have the best-looking movies possible. Many methods of compression are available, each with its own strengths. **Table 16.1** (opposite) provides an overview of the compressors available when exporting from iMovie. More are available if you export files from QuickTime Player Pro, and still more are offered by professional editing packages such as Apple's Compressor (part of Final Cut Studio) or Cleaner (www.autodesk.com/cleaner).

Data Rate: The amount of data sent from one point to another during a given time, such as the number of kilobytes delivered during a Web download.

Frame Rate: The number of frames displayed during 1 second. As more frames are included, the movie will play smoother—but adding frames increases the size of the file. Uncompressed DV video runs at 30 frames per second (fps) for NTSC, or 25 fps for PAL; a typical QuickTime movie contains 15 or 12 frames per second.

Key Frame: A complete movie frame that acts as the image base for successive frames. Unlike film, which displays 24 full frames per second on a reel of celluloid, QuickTime compares most of the frames in a movie with its key frames and notes the differences. Although this sounds like more work than just displaying each frame in its entirety, it actually means the movie player is drawing less data.

For example, consider a clip where the camera is stationary, filming a person talking. Every pixel of the first frame, the key frame, is drawn; in the next frame, the only change is that the person's lips have moved. Instead of redrawing the background and everything else, Quick-Time holds onto the first frame and only changes the pixels around the person's mouth. So, the second frame (and third, fourth, and so on) contain only a few pixels' worth of information, dramatically reducing the total amount of data required and creating a smaller file. Of course, the entire movie likely won't be composed of just the person talking, so QuickTime creates several key frames along the way, allowing the player to regroup and start over. The more key frames that appear in your movie, the larger the file size will be.

Sample Rate: The quality of audio, measured in kilohertz (kHz). The higher the number, the more audio data is present, and therefore the better the quality of sound.

Table 16.1

Video Compressors Included with QuickTime*	
COMPRESSOR NAME	COMMENTS
Animation	Works best on computer-generated animations with broad areas of flat color. Doesn't work well for scenes with lots of color changes.
Apple H.263, VC.263	Originally designed for videoconferencing. Very high compression ratios. Sometimes good for Web video.
Apple Pixlet Video	A low file size format developed by Apple and Pixar for desktop editing of high-resolution footage.
BMP	Used for still images to be exported in BMP format. Does minimal compression. Inappropriate for video-based movie playback.
Cinepak	Commonly used for video movies that require CD-ROM playback. Compresses very slowly.
Component Video	High-quality compressor. Good for capture on Macs with built-in video capture capabilities and for use as an intermediate storage format. Low compression ratios (larger files).
DV-PAL, DV/DVCPRO-NTSC, DVCPRO-PAL	Used with digital video cameras.
Graphics	Good for 8-bit graphics files. Usually better than the Animation compressor in 8 bits. Slower to decompress than Animation.
H.261	Originally designed for videoconferencing. Extremely high compression ratios.
H.264	A high-quality, scalable video format included with QuickTime 7 (and available under Mac OS X 10.4 Tiger or later). H.264 is designed to run on devices as varied as cellular phones and high-definition televisions, and is the backbone of upcoming HD DVD formats.
JPEG 2000	High image quality and resolution for still images, using wavelet compression.
Motion JPEG A, Motion JPEG B	Used to decompress files made with certain Motion JPEG cards when the card isn't available or to compress in a format that can be played by certain hardware Motion JPEG cards.
MPEG-4 Video	High quality compressed video based on QuickTime.
None	Good for capture only. Does almost no compression.
Photo-JPEG	Ideal for high-quality compressed still images. Also useful as an intermediate storage format for movies and QuickTime VR panoramas. Decompresses too slowly for video-based playback.
Planar RGB	For images with an alpha channel.
PNG	Typically used for still-image compression. Can get high compression ratios.
Sorenson Video 2	Very high compression ratios and high quality. Excellent for Web and CD-ROM.
Sorenson Video 3	Very high compression ratios and very high quality (better than Sorenson Video 2). Currently the best choice for Web and CD-ROM.
TIFF	Typically used for still-image compression. Does minimal compression.
Video	Very fast video compression and decompression. Decent compression ratios. Good for real-time capture of video, particularly when hard disk space is at a premium. Good for testing clips. OK for hard disk playback. Image quality is poor when compressing enough for CD-ROM playback.

Note: The Minimum Install of QuickTime (which many users will choose) doesn't install all these compressors. If the computer being used to play a movie that requires one of these compressors has an Internet connection, QuickTime downloads the necessary compressor when it is needed for decompression.

* This table has been adapted from one that originally appeared in *QuickTime 5 for Macintosh and Windows: Visual QuickStart Guide*, by Judith Stern and Robert Lettieri, and is used here with their permission. (www.judyandrobert.com)

EXPORTING TO QUICKTIME

To prepare a movie for Internet streaming:

1. Share your movie as described in the previous steps.

2. In the Movie Settings dialog, click the Prepare for Internet Streaming box in the lower-left corner (**Figure 16.7**).

3. From the popup menu, select a streaming method:

    ▲ **Fast Start.** The movie file is downloaded like any other media file, and begins playing once enough data has been transferred.

    ▲ **Fast Start - Compressed Header.** Like Fast Start, the movie is downloaded as one file, but the header information is compressed to save disk space.

    ▲ **Hinted Streaming.** Use this option if the movie will be hosted by a QuickTime Streaming Server. Hinting the data breaks it up into more manageable chunks for streaming. With Hinted Streaming selected, you can click the Settings button to further tweak the settings (**Figure 16.8**). For more information, see Apple's article: http://docs.info.apple.com/ article.html?artnum=301355.

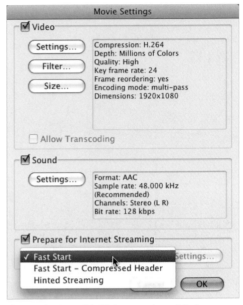

Figure 16.7 To enable Web streaming, click the Prepare for Internet Streaming box and choose a streaming method.

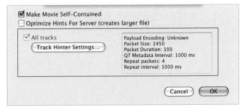

Figure 16.8 Preparing a QuickTime movie for streaming can get into a lot of geeky detail, but if you know what you're doing, you can improve streaming quality.

QuickTime Geekery

Trust me: Everything described so far in this chapter is really just the tip of a very large iceberg. If you're willing to shell out the bucks, software such as AutoDesk's Cleaner can encode and compress your movies into nearly any possible movie format, with more control than can be found in iMovie's or QuickTime Player's export features.

Figure 16.9 Create an XML file for Final Cut of your project that details all of the edits.

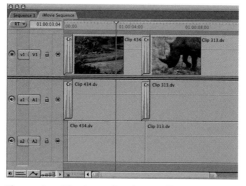

Figure 16.10 After importing the XML file into Final Cut Pro, your clips appear on the Timeline for editing.

Exporting Final Cut XML

For some people, iMovie is just the first step in editing video. Because it's designed for building movies quickly, iMovie is often used to throw together a rough assembly; from there, the movie is sent to Final Cut Pro for refinement.

Rather than rely on Final Cut Pro to parse iMovie's file format, iMovie does the work ahead of time by creating an XML (eXtensible Markup Language) file compatible with Final Cut Pro. That file is a simple text file that tells Final Cut which edits are applied and where—you can open it in a text editor and see for yourself.

To export Final Cut XML:

1. Select the project you want to export in the Project List.

2. Choose Export Final Cut XML from the Share menu.

3. In the dialog that appears, choose a destination and enter a name for the XML file that will be created (**Figure 16.9**).

4. Click Save to build the XML file.

   After importing the file into Final Cut Pro, the video is ready for further editing (**Figure 16.10**).

✔ Tip

■ If you know you're going to end up in Final Cut Pro, don't bother making the movie pretty. All transitions are converted to the cross dissolves, audio not embedded in the video is ignored, and cropping and color adjustments also don't make the trip.

Exporting to a Palm OS Handheld

A friend recently bought a Palm OS hand-held with a color screen so she could show off digital photos of her grandchildren. Now, she can also store movies by exporting them in QuickTime format and running them through Kinoma Producer (www.kinoma.com).

To export movies to a Palm OS handheld:

1. Make sure you've installed Kinoma Producer and Kinoma Player on the handheld.

2. In iMovie, export your movie using the QuickTime options. Kinoma recommends using the highest resolution possible, so start with iMovie's Full Quality export option.

3. Launch Kinoma Producer and choose your handheld model from the Brand and Model popup menus (**Figure 16.11**).

4. Drag your exported QuickTime movie to the Files area in Kinoma Producer, or click the Add Files button and locate the movie (**Figure 16.12**).

5. Click the Convert Files button.

6. After the conversion is finished, copy the new file to your handheld. Depending on the size of the movie file, you'll probably need to store it on a memory card instead of the handheld's built-in memory; I use a USB card reader to quickly transfer the file to the memory card. Be sure to copy it to the PALM > PROGRAMS > KINOMA folder.

7. Launch Kinoma Player and play the movie on your handheld (**Figure 16.13**).

Figure 16.11 In Kinoma Producer, choose your handheld's brand and model to begin.

Figure 16.12 Add QuickTime movies you exported from iMovie to Kinoma's Files pane.

Figure 16.13 Play back the movie on the handheld using Kinoma Player, and impress your friends with your tech savvy.

Part 4
iDVD

MOVING FROM iMOVIE TO iDVD

My father had amassed a pretty large videotape collection over the past several years. So you can imagine he did a fair bit of eye-rolling as DVD discs quickly gained in popularity, because now he needs to build a DVD collection, too.

DVD has several key advantages over VHS. The discs are smaller than videotapes, their image and sound quality are much better, and discs don't degrade over time (at least, not remotely as fast as tape, a fact you're no doubt aware of if you have an aging wedding or graduation video). And DVDs are inter-active: jump to your favorite scene in a movie; store several movies on one disc that can be accessed without fast-forwarding.

And yet, in Apple's eyes the DVD is already on its way out, expecting that soon everyone will be turning to the Web for distributing their movies. iMovie '08 removed a feature found in iMovie HD that let you create DVD chapter markers from within iMovie. That enabled you to set up chapters for the DVD. The capability still exists, just not within iMovie. Instead, take a side trip through GarageBand on the way to iDVD to create the chapters.

Creating Chapter Markers in GarageBand

When you watch a feature movie on DVD, you usually have the option of skipping to specific scenes, or chapters. You can set up chapter markers in GarageBand that iDVD imports as chapters.

To create chapter markers:

1. To get the movie out of iMovie, share it with the Media Browser at the Large size (see Chapter 15).

2. Launch GarageBand and create a new project.

3. Choose Show Media Browser from the Control menu. The browser appears at the right edge of the window.

4. Click the Movies button and expand the iMovie item to view your projects.

5. Drag the shared movie to the Timeline to add it to the project. It appears on a new video track.

6. Place the Playhead at the point that you'd like to set as a marker. Use the movie preview as a guide, not the thumbnails in the Movie Track.

7. Choose Add Marker from the Edit menu, or press the P key; a yellow diamond appears above the track (**Figure 17.1**). Repeat this step for as many markers as you want to create.

To send the movie to iDVD:

◆ Choose Send Movie to iDVD from the Share menu. GarageBand prepares the movie, opens iDVD, and creates a new project with the movie already loaded (**Figure 17.2**).

Marker

Figure 17.1 A marker is created above the Movie Track.

Figure 17.2 The new iDVD project includes an option to play your entire movie (top), or you can access the chapters you created by double-clicking the Scene Selection option (result at bottom).

iDVD Overview

iMovie took a technology dominated by professionals—movie editing—and made it easy to use for normal people. In some ways, though, iDVD is even more impressive.

Quite a lot of highly technical work goes into creating a DVD—in the background. While you're focused on choosing which photo should appear on the title page of your DVD, iDVD handles the specifics of building the structure necessary for most consumer DVD players to play back your masterpiece. More importantly, it manages the MPEG-2 compression needed to cram multiple gigabytes' worth of data onto a shiny platter the size and shape of a regular audio CD.

iDVD also does something that no other program can do: It gives you style. Apple has clearly put a lot of thought into the DVD themes that ship with iDVD, making each one something you'd actually want to show off to people. An iDVD project, whether you like it or not, is *polished*, which goes a long way toward making people think, "Wow, I had no idea he was so talented."

This chapter offers a look at iDVD's interface and major functions in order to give you the foundation you'll need for the next chapters that deal with building projects and customizing them.

HD and iDVD

iMovie can create HD movies, but don't expect to create a high-definition DVD for now. No standard for high-def DVDs has been reached, despite two competing formats (Blu-ray and HD-DVD, which each have different corporate backers).

In the meantime, iDVD imports HD projects with ease and converts them into widescreen DV format. True, it's not the same as seeing the picture at high-definition quality, but it's a start.

About DVDs

The Digital Versatile Disc is quite a wonder: it's physically small, like a CD, but packs nearly seven times the data into the same space: a CD stores roughly 700 MB, while a DVD holds approximately 4.7 GB. In addition to storing all this data, DVDs can be set up so they automatically play movie files and include a menu system to give you control over how the content plays.

DVD physical formats

Before you rush out and buy a mega-pack of blank DVDs, take a few minutes to acquaint yourself with the different formats that are out there.

◆ **DVD-R.** DVD-Recordable discs can be burned once, and then played back in nearly any consumer DVD player and DVD-capable computer. When purchasing DVD-R media, be sure to get DVD-R (General); the other type, DVD-R (Authoring), is used in professional DVD writers and is not supported by iDVD. The discs Apple sells are DVD-R format.

◆ **DVD-RW.** DVD-Rewritable discs can be erased and burned hundreds of times, which make them great for testing purposes (you can burn iterations of your project onto one DVD-RW disc, instead of making lots of DVD-R coasters).

◆ **DVD+R, DVD+RW.** These two formats use a different method of recording data than DVD-R and DVD-RW. They don't offer more storage or features, and cost about the same as the -R and -RW discs.

◆ **DVD-ROM.** DVD-Read-Only-Media discs cannot be burned because their data has already been written to disc. The iLife installation disc is an example of DVD-ROM.

4x DVD Media Alert!

Before you burn any DVD disc, make sure your SuperDrive's firmware has been updated. All SuperDrives can burn 1x- and 2x-speed DVD-R media. When using 4x-speed media, however, some older mechanisms can not only fail to write the disc, but they can also be permanently damaged! Fixes are available—see `http://docs.info.apple.com/article.html?artnum=86130` for more information.

DVD Logical Structure

A blank DVD disc contains no information or directory structure. The way a DVD's data is stored on the disc depends on how the disc will be used.

◆ **DVD-Video.** A DVD that contains just a movie (and its associated menus and extras) is in DVD-Video format. The folders and filenames are specific: a folder called VIDEO_TS stores all of the movie's video and audio files. iDVD typically creates DVD-Video discs.

◆ **DVD-ROM.** When you store just data on the disc, without the need to play back automatically in DVD players, the disc is in DVD-ROM format. This is just like using a CD-ROM, only with more storage capacity. The Finder can create DVD-ROM discs, such as when you're backing up data.

◆ **Hybrid DVD.** You can store a DVD-Video project on a disc that also contains DVD-ROM data, which makes the disc a Hybrid DVD. iDVD can create Hybrid DVDs.

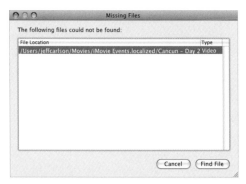

Figure 18.1 If iDVD cannot locate the media files used in your project, it displays this dialog.

Switch Between NTSC and PAL

Choose Project Info from the Project menu, and change the Video Mode setting at any time. Also, in iDVD's preferences you'll find a Video Mode setting in the Projects area that applies to new projects.

DVD Disc Speeds

DVD discs are marked as being 1x, 2x, 4x, or 8x speed. The SuperDrive that comes in the current iMac, for example, writes data at 8x speed, which means the laser that carves into the disc's surface is fast enough to keep up with a faster-spinning disc. All recent SuperDrives can write to higher-speed media, even if they're not 4x- or 8x-speed drives, at 1x or 2x speed.

Using iDVD on Non-SuperDrive Macs

You can run iDVD '08 on a Mac that does not include a SuperDrive, then archive your project or save it to a disc image for burning on another computer (see Chapter 22).

Working with iDVD Projects

If iDVD is currently running because you shared a movie from GarageBand, you don't need to open, create, or save your project—it's all done for you. If you just launched iDVD independently, you can create a new project or open an existing project from the File menu; doing so closes the current project (only one project can be open at a time).

The iDVD project file

The iDVD project file appears by default in your Documents folder (within your Home folder), and ends in the extension ".dvdproj". iDVD stores all of its related files in the project file itself, which is a *package*.

✔ Tips

- Many of the newest Mac models sport SuperDrives that burn dual-layer DVD media, which can store up to 8.5 GB of data and hold around three hours of video footage.

- Make sure you have plenty of free hard disk space available—at least 10 to 20 GB.

- Storing the project file in the Documents folder may be fine for casual use, but an iDVD project may not fit on your startup disk. When traveling, I move the project file to another partition of my PowerBook's hard disk, or offload everything to a speedy external drive.

- If you do move your iDVD project, make sure it can still locate your original iMovie project and its media files. If iDVD gets confused, it warns you with a dialog (**Figure 18.1**). Select a file from the list and click Find File if the file is actually available somewhere else, or click Cancel to proceed. You can still work on the project if you cancel, but you'll get a broken link warning if you play any of the footage.

Using OneStep DVD

Sometimes you may want to just burn some footage to a disc, without dealing with pretty graphics or navigation. Film productions frequently create DVD "dailies" of each day's footage for the director or producers to review; wedding videographers sometimes offer the raw footage to the married couple, handed over at the end of the day. iDVD's OneStep DVD feature simply grabs video from your camcorder and burns it to disc, with no menu navigation or frills. When you play it in a DVD player, the movie starts playing right away.

To create a OneStep DVD:

1. Connect your camcorder to your Mac and make sure it's loaded with the tape containing your footage.

2. Choose OneStep DVD from the File menu, or press the OneStep DVD button on iDVD's title screen (**Figure 18.2**).

3. Insert a recordable DVD disc into your computer.

4. Sit back and wait. iDVD rewinds the tape, imports the footage, encodes it, and burns it to the disc (**Figure 18.3**).

5. If you want another copy made after iDVD finishes, insert another disc. Otherwise, click Done.

✔ Tips

- OneStep DVD imports footage until it reaches the end of the tape or the end of the footage. If you want just a portion of the tape recorded, press the Stop button in iDVD or on the camcorder.

- You can't start importing footage in the middle of a tape using OneStep DVD. If you want to burn just a portion of your video, import it into iMovie first.

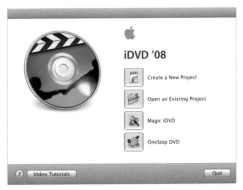

Figure 18.2 If no iDVD project is currently open, start a OneStep DVD project from the title screen.

Figure 18.3 OneStep DVD automatically rewinds the camera's tape, imports the footage (top), and burns a DVD disc (bottom).

OneStep DVD Data Location

When you use the OneStep DVD feature, iDVD doesn't create a project that you can go edit later. All OneStep DVD files are stored in a temporary, invisible directory on your startup drive. But you can change the location: open iDVD's preferences, click the Advanced icon, and choose a new temporary folder location (say, a larger hard disk) at the bottom of the window.

Figure 18.4 Think of Magic iDVD as the parent who gave you a helpful push when you first learned to ride a bicycle (without crashing into the neighbor's tree, in my case).

Figure 18.5 After you choose Create Project, edit the project as described in the upcoming chapters.

Using Magic iDVD

To get more of iDVD's style without spending a lot of time building a full project, drag movies, music, and photos from your hard disk onto the Magic iDVD interface and let iDVD do the work. You can then burn it straight to disc, or use the project as the jumping-off point for your own customizing.

To create a Magic iDVD project:

1. Choose Magic iDVD from the File menu, or press the Magic iDVD button on iDVD's title screen.

2. In the Magic iDVD window, type a name for your DVD in the DVD Title field (**Figure 18.4**).

3. Choose a theme from the scrolling list.

4. Click the Movies button to view movies (including iMovie projects) on your computer, and drag the ones you want to the Drop Movies Here area.

5. To include slideshows, click the Photos button and drag photos from your iPhoto library to the Drop Photos Here area. Each slot represents a different slideshow that can include several photos.

6. If you want music with your slideshow, click the Audio button and drag songs from your iTunes library to a slideshow.

7. Click the Preview button at any time to see what the project looks like.

8. Click the Create Project button to create a new project (**Figure 18.5**), or click the Burn button to write directly to a DVD.

✔ Tips

- You can also drag media content from the Finder to the Magic iDVD areas.

- To preview a song or movie, double-click it, or select it and press the Play button.

iDVD's Interface

Some software is deep, with lots of hidden, out-of-the-way features. iDVD is not one of those programs. That's not to say it isn't deep in what it can do—rather, it's easy to find what you need, quickly.

Menu/main window

iDVD's main window, referred to as the *menu*, displays the first set of options that your viewers will encounter (**Figure 18.6**). Choose between standard or widescreen modes, depending on the aspect ratio of your movie.

To switch format modes:

◆ From the Project menu, choose Switch to Standard (4:3) or Switch to Widescreen (16:9), or press Command-Option-A (**Figure 18.7**).

✔ Tips

■ The term "menu" is confusing in iDVD. Normally, a menu is a list of commands that you access from the menu bar at the top of the screen. In DVD parlance, however, a menu is the screen you're looking at. Think of it like a restaurant menu: the main window is a space to list the items (movies, etc.) you can select.

■ The widescreen format is designed to play on widescreen televisions without letterboxing the picture. All themes can be made widescreen (even old ones).

■ Switch between standard and widescreen layout at any time; you're not locked into one or the other.

■ Motion-enabled menus are generally processor-intensive, so I rarely leave the Motion button enabled while I edit.

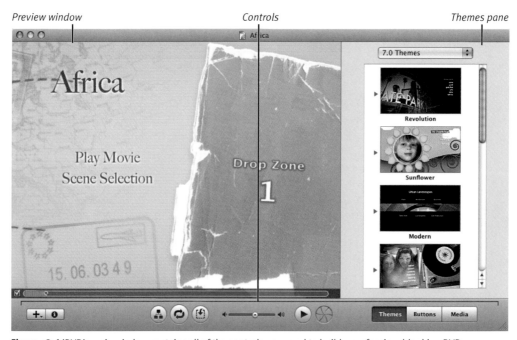

Preview window *Controls* *Themes pane*

Figure 18.6 iDVD's main window contains all of the controls you need to build a professional-looking DVD.

Standard (4:3)

Widescreen (16:9)

Figure 18.7 Work in standard or widescreen mode.

Important iDVD Interface Terms

◆ **Button.** Any interactive element in the DVD workspace is a *button*, even if it doesn't always look like a button. New movies, slideshows, and chapters are all buttons, because they require some sort of action on the part of the user to activate them.

◆ **Submenu.** The exception to buttons are *submenus*, which are containers that hold more stuff. An example of a submenu would be the "Scene Selection" option that appears when you import a movie with chapter markers. The item is a control that takes you to another menu screen, which includes buttons for each chapter that you've set up.

◆ **Theme.** A *theme* is the overall look of a menu screen, including the visual presentation (fonts, colors, etc.) as well as the way it interacts (with motion menus, etc.).

Controls

The program's main controls run below the preview window:

◆ **Add button.** Click this button to display a popup menu that lets you add a submenu, movie, or slideshow.

◆ **Inspector button.** Click to display the floating Inspector window.

◆ **Map button.** Click to see the Map view, which displays the project's content structure. You can organize the project's structure, assign themes to menus, and specify media that will start playing when a disc is begun, even before the first menu screen.

◆ **Motion button.** Click to toggle animation and movie previews, available for most iDVD themes. The Motion button turns them on or off while you're editing.

◆ **Edit Drop Zones button.** Click this button to display the Drop Zone editing interface in the main window.

◆ **Volume slider.** Set the volume of the theme elements (such as background music) while you're working; it doesn't affect the project's volume level.

◆ **Preview button.** Switch into preview mode to get a sense of how the DVD's menus and content will run.

◆ **Burn button.** Start the encoding and burning process to create a final disc.

◆ **Editing panes.** Clicking one of these buttons displays panes for editing the project's content.

✔ Tip

■ The iDVD window is also resizable. Choose Actual Size from the Window menu to go back to the native resolution.

Creating a New Project

Bringing in a movie from iMovie via Garage-Band isn't the only entryway to iDVD. You can start by creating a new empty project.

To create a new project in iDVD:

1. Choose New from the File menu, or click the Create a New Project button from iDVD's title screen. The Save As tdialog appears.

2. Give the project a name and choose where to save it.

3. Choose an aspect ratio, and then click the Create button (**Figure 18.8**).

To import video footage:

1. Click the Media button and then the Movies button to display the Movies list.

2. Drag a movie to the menu to add it (**Figure 18.9**).

Or

1. From the File menu, go to the Import submenu and choose Video.

2. Locate a video source, such as a Quick-Time movie, and click Import. A new button or submenu (depending on the movie) appears in the preview window for that video (**Figure 18.10**).

✔ Tip

■ You can also drag a QuickTime movie from the Finder to the iDVD window, but make sure you don't release it over a drop zone (see Chapter 19).

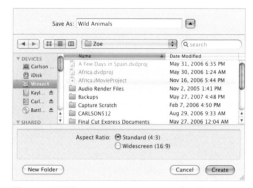

Figure 18.8 When you create a new project from scratch, choose a starting aspect ratio.

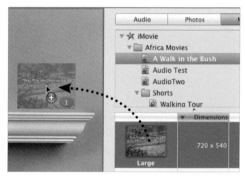

Figure 18.9 Drag items you've previously shared with the Media Browser.

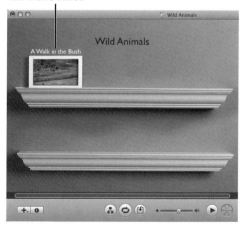

Figure 18.10 When you import a video to an iDVD project, it appears as a new menu item.

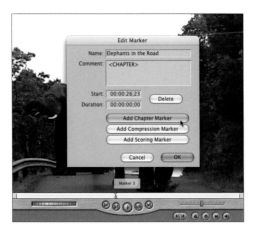

Figure 18.11 In Final Cut Express or Final Cut Pro, click the Add Chapter Marker button to ensure that iDVD will import the chapters correctly.

How to Add Chapters to an Existing iDVD Project

Although you can't create DVD chapter markers in iMovie '08, you can add them later in iDVD. Unfortunately, the feature is annoyingly limited. Instead of placing markers where you want them, iDVD can only create new chapter breaks every few minutes. Here's how:

To create chapter markers in iDVD:

1. Select a movie you've imported into your iDVD project.

2. Choose Create Chapter Markers for Movie from the Advanced menu.

3. In the dialog that appears, enter the number of minutes that pass between markers (such as "Create marker every 5 minutes").

4. Click OK. When you click the movie, it takes you to a submenu with options to play the full movie or jump to individual chapters.

Creating an iDVD Project from Final Cut

Video editors working in Final Cut Express or Final Cut Pro often bring their work into iDVD to create their DVD discs.

To export from Final Cut:

1. If you want to use Final Cut markers as iDVD chapter markers, be sure they're set up as such: Locate a marker and press M to bring up the Edit Marker dialog.

2. Click the Add Chapter Marker button (**Figure 18.11**). The text <CHAPTER> appears in the Comment field. Click OK.

3. From the File menu, choose QuickTime Movie from the Export submenu.

4. In the Save dialog, make sure Audio and Video is chosen from the Include popup menu.

5. Choose Chapter Markers from the Markers popup menu.

6. Click Save to save the file.

7. In iDVD, import the file as described on the opposite page.

Creating a Submenu

If you used GarageBand to set up chapter markers and create your iDVD project, your menu contains a Play Movie button that plays back the entire movie, and a button labeled Scene Selection. That second button is actually a *submenu* that branches off from the main menu. Double-clicking Scene Selection takes you to another menu screen that includes buttons to play chapters of your movie.

You can create new submenus that lead to other media—more movies or photos, for example.

To create a submenu:

1. Click the Add button and choose Add Submenu from the popup menu that appears. A new item named "My Submenu" appears (**Figure 18.12**).

2. Double-click the submenu name. The current theme is used for the new submenu, and includes a back arrow icon that, when clicked, leads to the main menu (**Figure 18.13**).

3. If you want, choose a different theme for the submenu.

To create a submenu in the Map view:

1. Click the Map button to switch to the Map view (**Figure 18.14**).

2. Select an icon for the menu where you want to add a submenu.

3. Click the Add button and choose Add Submenu. The new item appears in the project hierarchy attached to the menu (**Figure 18.15**).

New submenu created

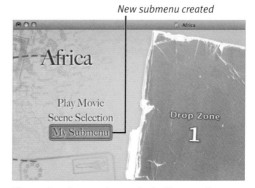

Figure 18.12 A new submenu looks like any other button in themes that use text buttons, but double-clicking it leads to a submenu.

Back button

Figure 18.13 The newly created submenu shares the previous menu's theme and is blank, except for a back arrow icon.

View top-down or left-to-right.   View icons smaller or larger using the size slider.

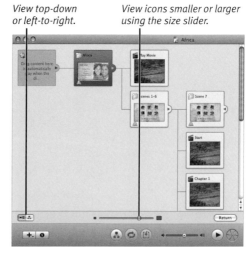

Figure 18.14 The Map view, once just a helpful snapshot, is now a useful tool in iDVD.

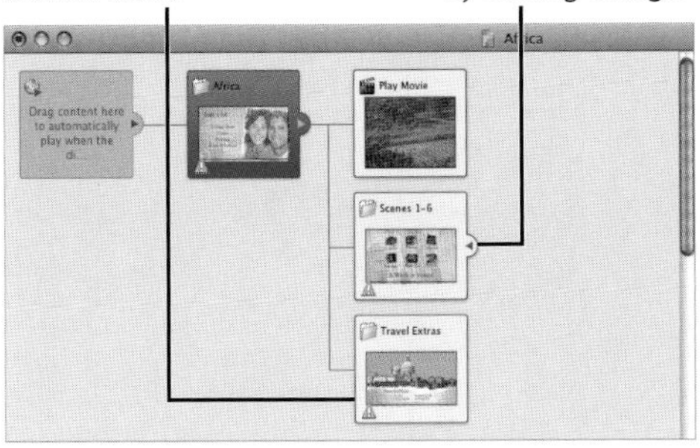

Submenu added to main menu   *Submenus hidden by clicking triangle*

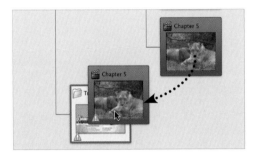

Figure 18.15 You can add submenus in the Map view.

Figure 18.16 One of my favorite features in iDVD is the ability to drag objects from page to page, or change the structure by dragging submenus to other menus.

To move objects to another submenu:

◆ Select an icon for a submenu, movie, or slideshow and drag it onto the icon for the submenu where the object will appear (**Figure 18.16**).

To delete a submenu:

1. Select a submenu's button (in the DVD menu) or icon (in the Map view).

2. Press the Delete key, or choose Delete from the Edit menu. The submenu disappears in a puff of smoke, as do any submenus, movies, or slideshows that it contained (but see the tip below).

✔ Tips

■ To delete a submenu but keep the objects that it contained, Control-click the submenu icon in the Map view and choose Smart Delete. Only the submenu is removed, leaving the other elements intact.

■ Want to move some menu items into their own submenu without creating the submenu separately? Select them and choose New Menu from Selection from the Project menu. A new submenu is created that contains the items. However, except for using Undo, note that you can't move them back to the main menu later if you decide they should have been there all along.

■ Click the small triangle to the right of a menu icon to hide or show lower-level items in the hierarchy (which is especially helpful when working on large, complicated projects).

■ Double-click an icon on the map to display the menu or play back the movie or slideshow. Clicking the movie or slideshow while it's playing takes you back to the Map view.

CREATING A SUBMENU

191

To use a transition between menus:

1. If you're currently within the submenu, click the back arrow icon to return to the previous menu. Transitions are applied to the menu that leads to the submenu.

2. Click the submenu's name or button to select it.

3. Click the Inspector button to display the floating Inspector.

4. Choose an effect from the Transition popup menu (**Figure 18.17**).

5. For transitions that move in more than one direction, such as Cube, choose a direction from the second popup menu under Transition.

6. Click the Preview button to see how your transition plays when you move between menus (**Figure 18.18**). (See "Previewing the DVD," later in this chapter.)

✔ Tips

■ Transitions can occur when switching between submenus, slideshows, and movies, but not when returning up through the hierarchy to the previous menu.

■ You can easily tell which menus include transitions by looking for a small blue circle to the left of their icons in the Map view.

■ Complex transitions can add to the time it takes to burn the disc.

Figure 18.17 Choose a type of transition to play when switching between menus.

Figure 18.18 Use the Preview mode to see how the transition plays (Mosaic Flip Small shown here).

CREATING A SUBMENU

Autoplay movie included

Figure 18.19 An icon in the upper-left corner of a theme's thumbnail image indicates an Autoplay movie.

Autoplay well

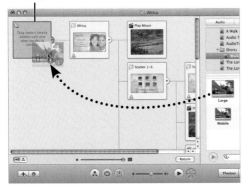

Figure 18.20 Drag a movie or photos to the Autoplay well to play them before the main menu appears.

Setting an Autoplay Movie

Nearly all of the commercial movie DVDs I've watched lately begin with either several screens of threatening information from various governmental agencies, or with some snazzy video animation or montage that plays before the main menu appears. In iDVD, this introductory material is known as an Autoplay movie, and is something you can create for your own projects. The Autoplay movie can be either a QuickTime movie or a slideshow. Themes with Autoplay movies include a special icon in their thumbnails (**Figure 18.19**).

To set an Autoplay movie:

1. Click the Map button to switch to the Map view. The icon in the upper-left corner is the Autoplay well.

2. Drag a movie file to the Autoplay well to set that as the Autoplay movie (**Figure 18.20**).

   You can also drag one or more photos, or an iPhoto album of photos, to the well, which turns them into a slideshow. To edit the contents of the slideshow, double-click the well (see Chapter 21).

To delete an Autoplay movie:

◆ Drag the contents of the Autoplay well outside the well. The media disappears with a poof.

✔ Tip

■ If you want to use an iMovie movie as the Autoplay movie, export it as Full Quality for the best image quality.

Previewing the DVD

The menu screen provides a good representation of what your viewers will see, but some aspects of a DVD—the way items are highlighted, for example—appear only when you preview the DVD. Obviously, you don't want to have to burn a new disc to see each iteration, which is why iDVD offers a preview mode.

To preview the DVD:

1. Click the Preview button to enter preview mode (**Figure 18.21**). A virtual DVD remote control appears.

   Using the remote, test the following features:

   ▲ Use the arrow keys, mouse pointer, or the arrow navigation buttons on the virtual remote control to move the button highlight between items (**Figure 18.22**).

   ▲ Use the forward and back buttons on the remote control to switch between chapters while watching the video.

   ▲ Click the Menu button to exit a movie and return to the movie's submenu, or click Title to return to the main menu.

2. Click the Exit button or the Stop button (with the square icon) to leave Preview mode.

✔ Tip

■ As you're previewing the project, pay attention to the order in which items are highlighted as you move the focus around the menu. Does it act the way a viewer would expect? Seeing the highlighting in action reminds me to re-arrange the order of my items. This is more important when your buttons don't align with the theme's invisible grid (see Chapter 20 for more on positioning items).

Button highlight   Remote control

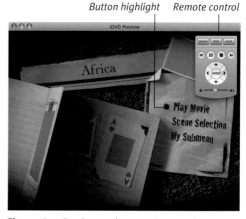

Figure 18.21 Preview mode approximates what your viewer will see when the DVD is played.

Previous chapter   Navigation buttons   Next chapter

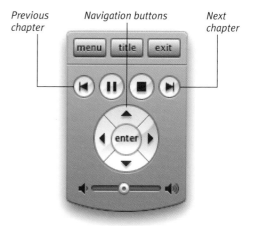

Figure 18.22 Even Apple's *virtual* remote controls are designed better than most real-world remotes.

Figure 18.23 The DVD-ROM Contents window is a blank canvas where you can add files that can be accessed by people viewing your DVD on a computer.

Figure 18.24 I find it easiest to just drag files and folders from the Finder to the DVD-ROM Contents window.

Adding DVD-ROM Data

Earlier in this chapter I mentioned that it's possible to create a hybrid DVD, which contains a DVD project as well as DVD-ROM files that can be read and copied using a Mac or PC. iDVD provides a straightforward (though slightly tucked away) method of adding files and folders to the disc.

To add files and folders to the DVD-ROM:

1. From the Advanced menu, choose Edit DVD-ROM Contents. The DVD-ROM Contents window appears (**Figure 18.23**).

2. Choose from the following options:
   - ▲ Click the New Folder button to create a new untitled folder.
   - ▲ Click the Add Files button to bring up an Open dialog where you can choose files to add.
   - ▲ Drag files or folders from the Finder onto the DVD-ROM Contents window (**Figure 18.24**).

3. Close the window when you're finished adding files and folders.

To remove DVD-ROM files and folders:

1. In the DVD-ROM Contents window, select one or more files.

2. Press the Delete key, or choose Delete from the Edit menu.

✔ Tips

- When you create an iDVD slideshow, you can choose to store copies of those photos on the DVD-ROM portion of the disc. If this option is enabled, the files will appear in the DVD-ROM Contents window, but they will be grayed-out and inaccessible. You'll need to turn off the option labeled Add image files to DVD-ROM to remove the files. See Chapter 21 for more information.

- Click and drag the files and folders in the window to change their order in the list. You can also move files into different folders, nest folders, or move everything to the same hierarchy.

- iDVD creates links to the files you've added to the DVD-ROM Contents window; it doesn't copy the files themselves until it's time to burn your disc. If you add a file or folder and then move its location on your hard disk, the item's name appears in red and you get a "File not found" message when you burn the DVD. Either move the file back to its original location (if you know it), or delete the reference in the DVD-ROM Contents window and add the file again.

- Apple recommends that you not use the DVD-ROM feature in iDVD to create system backups of your hard disk, because saving "more than a few thousand files may not work." Instead, use the disc burning features in the Finder, or better yet, create a backup system.

ADDING DVD-ROM DATA

19

iDVD THEMES

My wife is moderately addicted to several home decorating shows on TV, the ones where a designer takes over a room and the homeowners marvel at the transformation (okay, so maybe I've watched a few, too). It's amazing what a new window treatment and a fresh coat of paint can do to a room.

You might think that iDVD themes are nothing more than curtains to dress up your movies, but that would diminish the possibilities that a DVD theme offers. A theme gives your movie character, but more importantly, it provides a framework for the movie and other related media. Your DVD can contain several movies, slideshows of digital still photos, music, and animation.

In this chapter, I'll cover the basics of choosing one of iDVD's pre-made themes and working with its integrated elements, such as drop zones, motion menus, and editing text. In the next chapter, I'll get into the specifics of customizing a theme and tailoring it to your own tastes. Like decorating an otherwise functional room, working with iDVD themes can add some flair to the presentation of your movie.

Applying a Theme

When you start iDVD, a theme is already selected for you—either the first one in iDVD's list, or the one that was active the last time you used the program. Applying a different theme is simply a matter of clicking on a new one in the Themes pane. Your buttons and submenus are retained with the look of the new theme applied.

Themes are organized in families, so your project can share a consistent look while also providing variation among the menus (**Figure 19.1**).

To apply a theme family:

1. Click the Themes button to display the Themes pane, if it's not already visible.

2. Click a theme family icon to apply the theme to the current menu and any submenus based on it.

   ▲ If you're working in the Standard (4:3) aspect ratio, iDVD offers to switch to Widescreen (16:9) mode (**Figure 19.2**). Click Keep to leave the mode unchanged (unless you want to switch, of course).

   ▲ You may also see an Apply Theme Family dialog confirming that you want the theme to apply to all of the submenus attached to the current menu. Click OK.

   After a few seconds, the theme changes in the main window.

To apply an individual theme:

1. Click the Themes button to display the Themes pane, if it's not already visible.

2. Choose a theme from the list by clicking its thumbnail image. After a few seconds, the new theme is applied.

Expansion triangle   Theme family   Theme

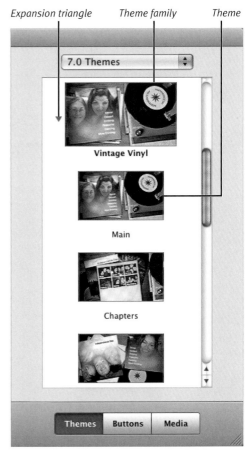

Figure 19.1 Click a theme in the Themes pane to apply it to your menu.

Figure 19.2 This dialog appears whenever you switch standard aspect ratio themes. Click the Do not ask me again checkbox to avoid it in the future.

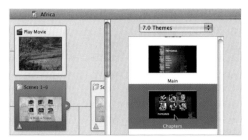

Figure 19.3 Select an icon in the Map view and then click a theme to apply it to that menu.

Before using Apply Theme to Submenus

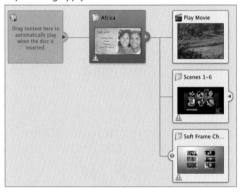

After using Apply Theme to Submenus

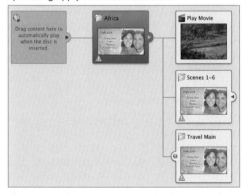

Figure 19.4 When you use the Apply Theme to Submenus command, all submenus are given the same theme. Looking at the Map view, you can see how the menus at the top use different themes. Afterwards, they all share the same theme.

To apply a theme in the Map view:

1. With the Themes pane visible, click the Map button.

2. Click the icon of the menu whose theme you want to change.

3. Click a theme from the Themes pane to apply the change (**Figure 19.3**).

4. Click the Return button to exit Map view.

To apply a theme to every menu in your project:

◆ In any menu screen, choose Apply Theme to Project from the Advanced menu. Every menu in your project now has the same theme.

To apply a theme to submenus:

1. Navigate to a submenu that you wish to change (the Map is a good place to do this; click the Map button, then click the menu you wish to view).

2. Choose Apply Theme to Submenus from the Advanced menu. The theme of every submenu in the current hierarchy is changed (**Figure 19.4**).

✔ Tips

■ Click the popup menu in the Themes pane to select themes from other versions of iDVD (or choose All to view them all in the list).

■ Feel free to mix and match themes within a family; for example, you can use the Extras theme in place of Chapters if you prefer.

■ You can purchase more custom themes from third party developers such as iDVD ThemePak (see Appendix B).

APPLYING A THEME

Using Motion

Menu items are designed to do more than display a text title or static image. DVDs typically convey video, so why not add some motion to the menus as well?

iDVD uses two types of motion: *motion menus*, which incorporate animated backgrounds, and *motion buttons*, which play movies or abbreviated photo slideshows in place of a generic button icon or still image. (Actually, there's also a third type of motion, audio, which is covered in the next chapter.) Most of iDVD's recent themes incorporate motion because it brings life to menus and makes them more than just pretty pictures.

In this section I cover motion buttons; see "Changing the Background" in Chapter 20 for details on using motion menus.

To activate motion:

◆ Click the Motion button, choose Motion from the Advanced menu, or press Command-J. The Motion button becomes highlighted in blue (**Figure 19.5**), and any animated elements within the theme, such as the background, drop zone, or submenu icons, start to play.

Perform any of the above actions to turn motion off.

✔ Tip

■ Turn off Motion when you're done editing the motion properties of your menu to improve performance while editing other aspects of your project.

Figure 19.5 Click the Motion button to activate the motion elements within the menu.

The Introductory Animation

Many themes include an introductory animation before the menu elements appear, indicated by a shaded section of the Motion Playhead scrubber bar (**Figure 19.6**). When the total animation finishes playing, it starts over where the vertical bar bisects the scrubber bar. To skip this first animation, deselect the checkbox to the left of the scrubber bar. Some themes also have a concluding animation, too.

Figure 19.6 The first section of the scrubber bar is the introductory animation, and isn't repeated.

Controls for these animations can also be found on the Menu Info window, marked Intro and Outro (**Figure 19.7**).

Figure 19.7 The Menu Info inspector also contains controls to enable the motion animations.

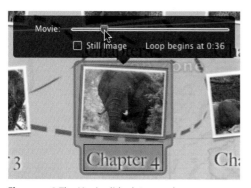

Figure 19.8 The Movie slider lets you choose a starting frame for your movie's button icon.

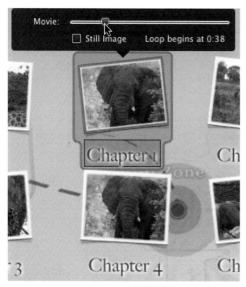

Figure 19.9 These two chapters appear in the same movie, which is why I can set the top chapter's button icon to match the bottom one (not that I'd want to, but you get the idea).

Motion buttons

Any QuickTime movie you add to your menu is a motion button—when motion is turned on, the movie plays within its button icon (except for themes that use only text as buttons, of course). Normally, the first frame of the movie button is the first frame of the movie itself; if you specified a poster frame for the movie file using QuickTime Pro (see Chapter 15), that frame is automatically set as the beginning. You can specify a new first frame, or choose not to play the movie at all and just use a frame of it as a still image.

To set the starting frame:

1. Click a motion button to select it, then click again or click and hold to display a Movie slider above it. (Be careful not to double-click the button, which plays the movie.) This works whether motion is activated or not.

2. Drag the Movie slider to locate the frame you wish to use as the starting point (**Figure 19.8**). Click outside the button to deselect it.

To turn off movie playback for a button:

1. Click a motion button and bring up the Movie slider.

2. Mark the Still Image checkbox.

3. Drag the slider to the frame you want to use as the thumbnail image.

✔ Tip

■ The chapters from a GarageBand-generated iDVD project all belong to the full movie, so when you're changing the starting frame of the motion button, the slider represents the entire movie, not just that chapter (**Figure 19.9**).

Motion duration

The Loop Duration slider in the Menu Info window controls how long your motion elements play before they are reset to their starting points.

To set motion duration:

1. Click the Inspector button to view the Menu Info window.

2. Drag the Loop Duration slider to change the duration of the motion menu (**Figure 19.10**). The number to the right of the slider represents the total time required to play all motion elements on the menu.

✔ Tips

- What if you don't want any motion when you burn your project to disc? Set the Loop Duration to 00:00, and disable any motion button movies, and turn off any of a theme's introductory or ending animations.

- The maximum menu duration used to be 30 seconds in previous versions of iDVD. Now, it's limited by the length of the menu's background movie or audio, whichever is longest, up to 15 minutes. If one ends before the other, it loops to keep the motion effect going.

- One of my biggest gripes about DVDs is that they don't loop cleanly, either on my projects or commercial DVDs. The motion menu reaches the end and pauses briefly before starting over. However, one feature can help: In iDVD's preferences, click the General icon and enable the option labeled Fade volume out at end of menu loop (**Figure 19.11**).

Figure 19.10 The Loop Duration slider controls the amount of animation that plays before starting over.

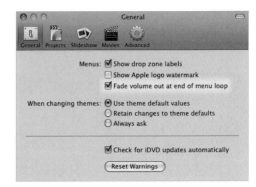

Figure 19.11 Tired of music getting chopped off at the end of a menu's animation? This preference will help.

Black and yellow border appears when media is over the drop zone.

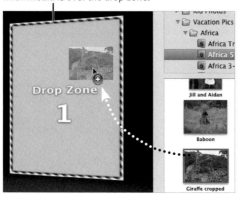

Figure 19.12 Drag a photo or movie from the Media pane to a menu's drop zone.

Drop Zone Movie Start/End

When you place a custom movie into a drop zone, you can control which portion of it plays during the menu's animation, just like editing the clip in iMovie. Click the movie in the drop zone to display the Movie Start/End control, and then drag the markers (**Figure 19.13**).

Drag to set start and end points in the drop zone.

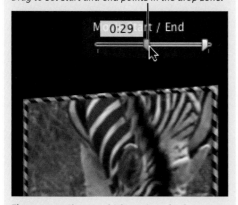

Figure 19.13 Choose which section of a drop zone movie plays in a menu's animation.

Using Drop Zones

To add a bit of visual interest and a personal touch to your menu, add a movie, photo, or collection of photos to the drop zones included with some themes.

To add a movie or photo to a drop zone:

1. Click the Media button to display the Media pane.

2. Click the Photos or Movies button at the top of the pane.

3. Drag a movie, photo, or multiple selected photos to a drop zone, indicated by a yellow border (**Figure 19.12**). iDVD adds the media to that zone.

Or

◆ Drag a movie or photo file(s) from the Finder to the drop zone.

Or

1. Click the Drop Zone Editor button to display the editor in the preview area.

2. Drag a movie, photo, or multiple selected photos to a drop zone placeholder.

Or

1. Control-click the drop zone and choose Import from the contextual menu.

2. In the Open dialog that appears, locate a movie or photo file on your hard disk, then click the Import button.

To remove media from a drop zone:

◆ Control-click the zone and choose Clear Drop Zone Contents from the contextual menu.

◆ Drag the photo or movie out of the drop zone and release the mouse button.

Working with dynamic drop zones

Some of the latest themes feature dynamic drop zones: one or more drop zones animated within the theme. Individually, they operate as normal drop zones, but you can also control them as a group.

Figure 19.14 The Drop Zone Editor is an easier way to add movies and photos to multiple drop zones.

To add movies or photos to dynamic drop zones:

1. Click the Edit Drop Zones button to view the Drop Zones editor (**Figure 19.14**).

2. Drag movies or photos to each drop zone.

3. Click the close button at the upper left corner to go back to the menu.

Or

1. Turn off Motion, if it's currently active, by clicking the Motion button. (You can leave it on if you want, but that makes it difficult to add each media item.)

2. Drag a movie or photo to a drop zone; each zone is numbered.

3. Advance the Motion Playhead by dragging it to the right (**Figure 19.15**). (If you don't see it, choose Show Motion Playhead from the View menu.) The animation progresses, revealing more drop zones.

4. Repeat steps 2 and 3 until you've populated the drop zones.

Figure 19.15 Drag the Motion Playhead to the right to advance through the dynamic drop zone animation.

Figure 19.16 Let iDVD randomly choose content for your drop zones.

Figure 19.17 Press the Command or Option key before you drop a media file to direct how it will be added.

To autofill drop zones:

1. Choose Autofill Drop Zones from the Project menu, or press Command-Shift-F.

2. Click the Autofill button. iDVD collects media that you've already used in the project (such as movies added) and fills the drop zones.

To fill a drop zone with content from your project:

◆ If you want to let iDVD do the choosing for you, Control-click a drop zone and choose Fill with Content (**Figure 19.16**). iDVD fills it with a movie or photo from your project.

✔ Tips

■ Consider waiting until you've added more content to your project before using the autofill feature, so that iDVD will have plenty of media to choose from.

■ The drag-and-drop approach can be problematic if your aim is poor: a few pixels off and you could find yourself replacing the menu's background image (see "Changing the Background" in Chapter 20). To ensure you're performing the action you want, press the Command or Option key when dragging to view a contextual menu with options for placing the media (**Figure 19.17**).

■ You can opt to turn off the "Drop Zone" text in iDVD's General preferences by disabling the Show drop zone labels checkbox. If you turn it off, the words reappear when you drag media onto the menu area.

Working with multiple photos in a drop zone

When you drag multiple photos to a drop zone, they act as a slideshow within the zone. You can change the order in which they appear, or add and delete photos using the Drop Zone Editor.

To set which photo displays first:

1. Click the zone to make it editable (**Figure 19.18**).

2. Drag the Photos slider that appears above the drop zone to choose a photo. That picture will appear first when the menu plays with motion.

To change the order of the photos:

1. Click the zone to make it editable.

2. Click the Edit Order button, or double click the drop zone. The Drop Zone Photos editor appears (**Figure 19.19**).

3. Drag the photos to change their order. iDVD numbers each icon to indicate the playback order.

4. Click the Return button to go back to the menu.

To add more photos:

1. Double-click the drop zone to display the Drop Zone Photos editor.

2. Drag more images from the Media pane or from the Finder.

3. Click the Return button to go back to the menu.

✔ Tip

- Click the view preference buttons in the upper-right corner of the Drop Zone Photos editor to display the photos either as thumbnails or as a list (with filenames).

Figure 19.18 Choose a different photo to appear in the drop zone by moving the Photos slider.

Figure 19.19 The Drop Zone Photos editor displays the photos you've added to the zone and their playback order.

USING DROP ZONES

Figure 19.20 Images 21, 27, and 32 are selected and ready to be deleted (or moved; see Chapter 21).

Figure 19.21 If you'd prefer to not include any drop zone content, disable them in the Menu Info window.

To delete photos from the drop zone:

1. In the Drop Zone Photos editor, select the photos you wish to remove. Shift-click to select a range of photos, or Command-click to select non-contiguous photos (**Figure 19.20**).

2. Press the Delete key or choose Delete from the Edit menu. The pictures are removed.

3. Click the Return button to go back to the menu (or the drop zone list).

To turn off drop zones entirely:

1. Click the Inspector button to display the Menu Info window.

2. Uncheck the option labeled Show drop zones and related graphics (**Figure 19.21**).

✔ Tips

■ iDVD determines the amount of time a photo appears depending on the number of photos you've given it. The more photos you add, the less time they stay onscreen. The overall time is based on the Loop Duration setting in the Menu Info window (see "Using Motion," earlier in this chapter).

■ If you've already added photos in the menu, dragging more to the drop zone replaces the ones you have; it doesn't add them to the existing lineup. Use the Drop Zone Photos editor to add more pictures.

■ It's not possible to resize or crop photos in a drop zone within iDVD, unfortunately. Some themes determine the size of the media by fitting the width of the photo or movie; others base the size on the height.

USING DROP ZONES

207

Editing Text

Not all text needs to be in service of buttons or submenus—edit and add your own text boxes. The following steps apply to changing the contents of text blocks; in the next chapter, I'll cover more settings such as changing the font and style.

To edit text:

1. Click once to select a button or title, and then click again to select the text (**Figure 19.22**). Don't *double-click* the button, however, because that will either play its movie or take you to a submenu.

2. Type your text. Hit Return or Enter to break the line (**Figure 19.23**).

3. Click outside the text field to deselect it and accept your changes.

To add new text:

1. Choose Add Text from the Project menu, or press Command-K. A new text block appears (**Figure 19.24**).

2. Edit the text as described above.

3. Position the text by dragging it where you want it; unlike the default behavior of buttons and menu titles, which snap to an invisible grid, a new text block can be placed anywhere on the screen. (See the next chapter for more on positioning buttons.)

✔ Tip

■ If the Inspector window is visible, the font formatting controls do not appear beneath the text.

To delete text:

1. Click a text block once to select it.

2. Press the Delete key, or choose Delete from the Edit menu. The text vanishes.

Figure 19.22 Click a button twice (but don't double-click) to edit its text.

Figure 19.23 Create multi-line text boxes by pressing Return or Enter.

Figure 19.24 Add text blocks that aren't buttons or submenus.

TV Safe Area   *Area likely to be cut off*

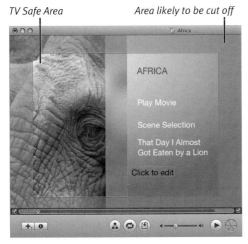

Figure 19.25 Items placed outside the safe area may get cropped out when played back on a television.

Standard Crop Area

Figure 19.26 The edges of widescreen projects can get hacked off by standard-definition TVs, but it won't matter if you use the Standard Crop Area indicator to position your text.

To insert special characters:

1. Click a text block once to select it, then click again to edit it.

2. Choose Special Characters from the Edit menu. The Character Palette appears.

3. Select the character you want to use in the palette.

4. Click the Insert button to add the character to your text.

✔ Tips

■ Some televisions don't display everything that you see in iDVD's screen. To make sure your text will appear, choose Show TV Safe Area from the View menu, or press Command-T, and position the text and buttons within the area that's not shaded (**Figure 19.25**).

■ If you're working in widescreen mode, choose Show Standard Crop Area from the View menu, or press Command-Option-T, to see where a standard-definition television showing a full-screen image will crop your menu (**Figure 19.26**).

CUSTOMIZING iDVD THEMES 20

The benefit of iDVD's approach to creating DVD menus is that everything is already in place; the background imagery, animation, typefaces, and navigation structure are all prefab. Your job is to fill in the content.

While that may sound nicely organized to some people, others see it as a collection of limitations. Where's the fun if everything is spelled out for you already? This is where iDVD's theme customization comes into play. It may not be as open-ended as Apple's professional-caliber DVD Studio Pro, but there's enough flexibility built in to let you make your own personal stamp on the menu design.

Editing Text Formatting

A hallmark of the Macintosh has been the capability to change the appearance of text onscreen. Sure, every computer now offers dozens of fonts and styles, but in 1984 that capability was a big deal. So it's sensible that you can change the font, alignment, and color of your menu titles, buttons, and text blocks.

To edit text formatting:

1. Click the text block you want to edit. If the Inspector window is not visible, a set of popup menus appears below the text (**Figure 20.1**). If the Inspector is visible, it becomes either the Text Info window or the Button Info window, depending on the text that's selected (**Figure 20.2**).

2. To change the text's font and size, use the following popup menus.

   ▲ **Family.** Choose a font family from this popup menu to change the font.

   ▲ **Typeface.** Choose the style of font from this popup menu.

   ▲ **Size.** Choose a font size from this popup menu.

3. With the Inspector window visible, you can also edit the following attributes:

   ▲ **Color.** Click the Color field to display the Colors palette and choose a new color (**Figure 20.3**).

   ▲ **Shadow.** Drop shadows are often overused in design, but in DVD menus they often make the text more readable. Click this checkbox to add a subtle drop shadow behind the text.

Figure 20.1 Change the formatting of the menu title or stand-alone text blocks in the Preview window.

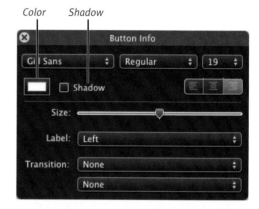

Figure 20.2 The Inspector window includes font formatting settings, but changes depending on what's selected: a button (top) or a text block, such as the menu's title (bottom).

Figure 20.3 iDVD uses the Mac OS X Colors palette to offer the full spectrum of colors.

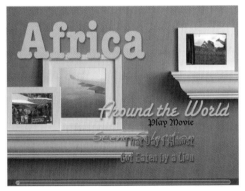

Figure 20.4 *Could* and *should* are two very different terms. *Restraint* is an even better word.

To reset text to the theme's default formatting:

1. Select the text block you want to change back to the theme's formatting.

2. Choose Reset Object to Theme Settings from the Advanced menu. Or, Control-click the block and choose Reset to Theme from the contextual menu.

✔ Tips

■ Hooray! In previous editions of this book, I've complained that you couldn't simply choose a standard font size (such as 12 point), but had to rely on an inaccurate slider. Now...you can.

■ More good news! iDVD lets you apply formatting changes to each text block or button label independently (**Figure 20.4**). The old restrictions of applying one font for all button labels is gone, gone, gone. However, remember that just because you *can* use all sorts of crazy fonts on your menu doesn't mean you *should*.

Editing Text Alignment and Position

iDVD uses two terms for aligning text: alignment and position. Alignment refers to how the text lines up within its allotted space, or how button labels appear in relation to each other. Position describes where a button's label appears in relation to the button's icon (if it's visible).

Title alignment

The title in each theme is bound to a specific area by default, but you can also opt to place it anywhere within the menu. You can also make it disappear if a title isn't needed.

To set the title alignment:

1. Select the menu title.

2. In the Inspector window, click one of the Align options: Left, Center, or Right (**Figure 20.5**). The text is moved relative to the area designated for the title. For example, choosing Center in the Reflection White theme shifts the text to the right of the default position; it doesn't move it to the center of the screen as you might expect (**Figure 20.6**).

   To position the text anywhere you want, simply drag the title elsewhere on the screen; doing so unlocks the title from the theme's placement grid and enables you to drag the title anywhere on screen (**Figure 20.7**).

To remove the menu title:

◆ Select the title and press the Delete key, or choose Delete from the Edit menu. Note that once a title has been deleted, you can't add it back to your page without using the Undo command.

Left   Center   Right

Figure 20.5 Choose an alignment button to specify text alignment.

Left alignment

Center alignment

Figure 20.6 A title's position is relative to the area allotted by the theme, not by the overall screen.

Custom positioning

Figure 20.7 You have the freedom to place the title anywhere.

EDITING TEXT ALIGNMENT AND POSITION

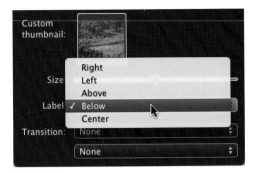

Below   *Center*

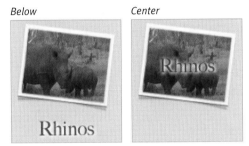

Figure 20.8 When a button includes an icon, the Position popup menu includes more options.

Aligned left

Aligned right

Figure 20.9 You can choose the alignment of text-only buttons.

Button label position

In themes where buttons include an icon, instead of just text, the Label popup menu determines where the text appears in relation to the icon.

To set the position of button text:

1. Select a button in the menu.

2. In the Button Info window, choose a button label location from the Label popup menu (**Figure 20.8**).

To remove button text:

1. Click the button to select it, then click it again to select the label's text.

2. Press the Delete key or choose Delete from the Edit menu.

Button text alignment

In themes that use only text for buttons, the Align controls specify the text alignment of the buttons relative to each other. (You can also switch normal buttons to text buttons on any theme; see "Editing Buttons" on the next page.)

To set the alignment of button text:

1. Select a text button in the menu.

2. In the Button Info window, click the Left, Center, or Right buttons to align the text of the labels to each other (**Figure 20.9**).

✔ Tip

■ Some label position settings don't work well in some themes. For example, using a Left Side position in some themes can make the text run off the screen or onto other buttons. You can move the buttons around, however; see "Editing Buttons" on the next page.

EDITING TEXT ALIGNMENT AND POSITION

Editing Buttons

Buttons are the mechanism by which your viewers interact with the DVD. In addition to changing the buttons' text, you can change their shape, location, and size, plus the highlight color.

To change the button style:

1. Select one or more buttons in the menu.

2. Click the Buttons button to view the Buttons pane. (By the way, now I can't stop saying "Buttons button!")

3. Choose a button type from the popup menu (**Figure 20.10**).

4. Click a button style to apply it to the selected button in the Preview window.

To reposition buttons:

◆ Drag a button onto another button to swap their locations on the grid. The others move out of your way as you drag.

◆ Drag the button to a new location within the menu (**Figure 20.11**). As you drag, iDVD displays alignment guides to help you line up objects.

Or

1. Select two or more buttons.

2. Control-click to bring up the contextual menu, and choose the options on the Align Objects and Distribute Objects submenus (**Figure 20.12**).

To re-align buttons:

1. With nothing selected in the Preview window, click the Inspector button to bring up the Menu Info window.

2. In the Buttons area, click Snap to Grid (**Figure 20.13**). The menu's buttons return to the layout grid.

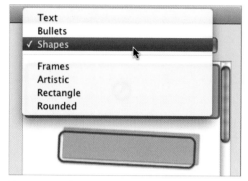

Figure 20.10 Change the appearance of button icons by choosing a new style in the Buttons pane.

Figure 20.11 You're free, to do what you want, any ol' time, by free positioning buttons.

Figure 20.12 Easily align and distribute buttons from the contextual menu.

EDITING BUTTONS

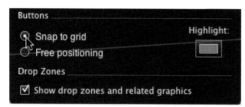

Figure 20.13 When it's time to crack down and restore order, click the Snap to grid radio button.

Figure 20.14 The Size slider makes button icons smaller or larger (but not the button text).

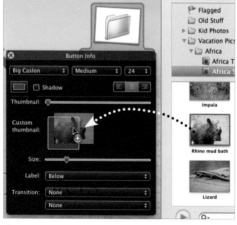

Figure 20.15 Drag a photo or movie from the Media pane to the Custom thumbnail field to change its icon (this works only in themes that use icons, naturally).

To change the button highlight color:

◆ In the Buttons area of the Menu Info window, click the Highlight field and choose a color from the Colors palette.

To resize buttons:

1. Select one or more buttons in the menu.

2. In the Button Info window, drag the Size slider. This feature becomes useful if you've added lots of buttons to your menu and you want to prevent overlap (**Figure 20.14**).

To change the appearance of a button icon:

◆ In themes with button icons, drag a photo or movie from the Media pane or the Finder onto the Button Info window's Custom thumbnail field (**Figure 20.15**). You can switch back to the generic sub-menu icon, if you want, by clicking the icon and moving the Thumbnail slider to the left. Or, drag the image out of the field to remove it. Only one photo or movie can be applied to a submenu icon—dragging others just replaces the previous image.

To reset a button to the theme default:

1. Select the button you want to change back to the theme's formatting.

2. Choose Reset Object to Theme Settings from the Advanced menu. Or, Control-click the block and choose Reset to Theme from the contextual menu.

✔ Tip

■ If you decide to position your buttons freely (without the grid), turn on the TV Safe Area (press Command-T or choose it from the Advanced menu) to make sure the buttons won't get cut off when viewed on some television screens.

Changing the Background

To alter a theme's appearance dramatically, swap the existing background image with your own photo or movie.

To use a photo or movie as the background:

1. Click either the Inspector button to bring up the Menu Info window or the Edit Drop Zones button.

2. Drag a photo or movie from the Media pane or the Finder and drop it onto the Menu icon in either location. The background image is replaced, but the drop zones remain (**Figure 20.16**).

Or

1. From the File menu, go to the Import submenu and choose Background Video.

2. Locate a movie on your hard disk, and click Import.

Or

1. Drag a photo or movie file from the Media pane or the Finder to the menu, but don't release the mouse button; be sure to avoid stopping on a drop zone.

2. Press the Command or Option key to bring up a contextual menu with choices (**Figure 20.17**).

3. Choose Replace background to use your file as the background.

To use a photo or movie as the background with no drop zones:

1. Follow the steps above to change the background image.

2. In the Menu Info window, deselect Show drop zones and related graphics (**Figure 20.18**).

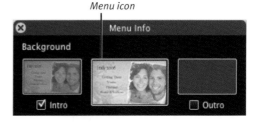

Menu icon

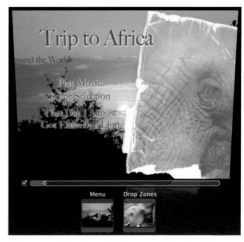

Figure 20.16 Adding a photo or movie to the Menu icon in the Menu Info window (top) or the Drop Zone Editor (bottom) makes it the theme's background.

Figure 20.17 Press Command or Option before releasing the mouse button to choose an action.

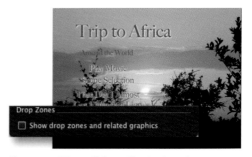

Figure 20.18 Turn off the option to show drop zones to use only your image or movie as the background.

Click this triangle to view the Start/End control.

Figure 20.19 Use the almost-secret control in the Loop Duration slider to set the start and end of your background video.

Figure 20.20 Drag a photo or movie file out of the Background well to revert to the theme's original background image. The image disappears in a poof of smoke. (I'm sure the more appropriate term is "puff" of smoke, but this seems more like a "poof.")

To set the beginning and ending of a background video:

1. With a video set as the background, make the Menu Info window visible.

2. Click the small triangle above the Loop Duration slider to display the Background Movie Start/End control (**Figure 20.19**). The triangle appears only when a video is used as the background.

3. Drag the ends of the control to set the start and end of the video.

To remove your background photo or movie:

1. Bring up the Drop Zone Editor or the Menu Info window.

2. Drag the photo or movie out of the Background well (**Figure 20.20**). The theme's default background reappears.

✔ Tips

- For best image quality, share your background movie from iMovie at the large setting (see Chapter 15).

- If the movie is meant as a visual item only, export it from iMovie with the sound disabled, or set at a low volume.

- If you switch to a different theme, your background image or movie is deleted from the project; you'll need to re-import it under the new theme.

- Remember that you won't see your movie in action unless Motion is enabled.

- If you remove a video from the background well, also be sure to remove the audio that the video may have added (see the next page).

- Import video files you shot with a digital still camera by locating them in the Media pane's Photos list.

CHANGING THE BACKGROUND

Setting Background Audio

Being a more visual person, I tend to forget about audio unless it's either (a) highly annoying, or (b) eerily nonexistent. Some themes include background audio, others don't, but you can add an audio file to any of them to customize your menu's sound.

To choose an audio file:

1. Switch to the Media pane, and click the Audio button (if it's not already active). Your GarageBand songs and iTunes music appear (**Figure 20.21**).

2. Locate the audio file you wish to use. To help narrow your search, click one of the playlists in the upper portion of the window, or type a name (song or artist) in the search box at the bottom.

3. Click the Play button if you want to preview the file. Otherwise, click the file to select it.

To add background audio:

◆ Drag an audio file from the Media pane or the Finder to the Audio well in the Menu Info window (**Figure 20.22**).

◆ Drag an audio file from the Media pane or the Finder to the Menu icon in the Drop Zone Editor.

◆ Drag an audio file from the Media pane or the Finder to the menu.

Or

1. From the File menu, choose Audio from the Import submenu.

2. Locate an audio file on your hard disk, and click Import.

To change audio's volume:

◆ Drag the Menu Volume slider in the Menu Info window.

Figure 20.21 The Audio list in the Media pane displays your iTunes and GarageBand songs.

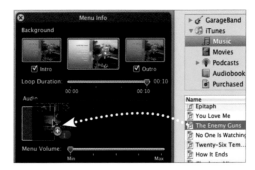

Figure 20.22 Drop a song file onto the Audio well to use that as your background sound.

Protected audio file

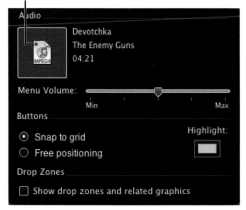

Figure 20.23 The icon in the Audio well can tell you if you're using protected audio content.

To remove background audio:

1. Bring up the Menu Info window or the Drop Zone Editor.

2. Drag the sound file out of the Audio well (or Menu well in the Drop Zone Editor). The well's icon changes to a generic speaker icon.

✔ Tips

- To play more than one song in the background, select multiple audio files and drag them to the Audio well together.

- If you want the background audio turned down, not off, use the Volume slider at the bottom of the iDVD window. This setting only affects the volume while you work, not the volume of the audio when the project is burned to disc.

- Background audio doesn't need to be music. Spoken-word content or other sound effects work just as well.

- You can drag a QuickTime movie to the Audio well and use only its audio track.

- GarageBand songs need to be saved with an iTunes preview before you can add them to iDVD (see Chapter 14).

- Speaking of GarageBand, that type of audio is great for a DVD menu: you have control over the duration of the song, and it can loop in the background.

- If you add a background movie, then delete the movie from the Background well, the audio stays. You also need to delete the music from the Audio well.

- iDVD recognizes when it's using protected audio files, such as songs you buy from the iTunes Music Store, and displays the file's icon (which includes a small lock image, **Figure 20.23**).

Looping Movie Playback

Normally, a movie or scene plays its frames and finishes, moving on to the next scene or returning to the menu. However, you can opt to loop a movie so that once started it will replay until you intervene.

To loop a movie:

1. Click the Map button to switch to the Map view.

2. Select a movie file.

3. Choose Loop Movie from the Advanced menu. A loop icon appears on the movie clip (**Figure 20.24**).

✔ Tips

- When you loop a movie chapter that's part of a larger movie, all of its chapters include the loop icon and the entire movie loops, not an individual chapter.

- This may be too obvious, but never loop an AutoPlay movie. If you do, the DVD will never proceed to the main menu.

- Did I say *never*? Looping the AutoPlay movie might be what you want if you're creating a video that needs to keep playing in a kiosk mode (such as for a convention booth, art installation, or other presentation).

Loop icon

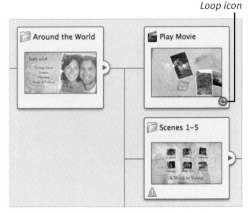

Figure 20.24 A loop icon in the Map view indicates that a movie will replay once it reaches its end.

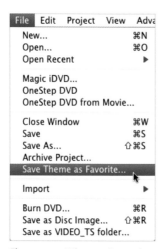

Figure 20.25 When you're ready to save your theme, choose the Save Theme as Favorite option.

Figure 20.26 Type a name for your new favorite theme, and decide if all users of your Mac can use it.

Favorite icon

Figure 20.27 Saved themes appear in the Themes pane's Favorites list, and include a custom icon.

Saving a Favorite Theme

You've added a new background, new music, and tweaked the buttons and text to your liking. If you want to keep this setting for future projects, save it as a favorite.

To save a favorite theme:

1. Choose Save Theme as Favorite from the File menu (**Figure 20.25**).

2. In the dialog that appears, type a name for the theme (**Figure 20.26**).

3. To make the theme available for all users on your computer, enable the Shared for all users option.

4. If you're changing a favorite that you've already created and want to save over it, mark the Replace existing checkbox.

5. After the theme is saved, it becomes available in the Themes pane. Choose Favorites or All from the popup menu to view your theme (**Figure 20.27**).

✔ Tips

■ If you've arranged your buttons with the Free Positioning option selected in the Menu Info window, those positions become the basis for the grid when you apply your favorite theme to a new project.

■ If you placed a photo or movie in a drop zone before saving the theme as a favorite, that media becomes part of the background image, but leaves the drop zone open for new media.

Deleting a Favorite Theme

Creating a favorite theme is a simple operation, but iDVD offers no similarly direct method of removing a favorite. However, you can do it with a little poking around in the Finder.

To delete a favorite theme:

1. Quit iDVD if it is running.

2. In the Finder, locate iDVD's Favorites folder. There are two; the location of the one you want to delete depends on whether the theme was made available to all users or not.

   ▲ If you enabled the Shared for all users option, go to [Computer] > Users > Shared > iDVD > Favorites (**Figure 20.28**).

   ▲ If you did not enable Shared for all users, go to Home > Library > Application Support > iDVD > Favorites (**Figure 20.29**).

3. Select the file corresponding to the theme you wish to delete, and drag it to the Trash.

4. Re-launch iDVD to see that the favorite theme is now no longer available.

Figure 20.28 A favorite theme shared by all users appears in Mac OS X's Users directory.

Figure 20.29 If the theme will be used only by you, it's stored within your user Library folder.

21

SLIDESHOWS

Most of this book centers on video and all of the wonderful things you can do with it. But your digital lifestyle probably includes a lot of still photos, too (either taken with a digital still camera or your camcorder, or scanned from paper originals).

In addition to providing a venue for your movies, iDVD can build slideshows from your photos, including transitions and audio, which can be played back on DVD players.

Creating a Slideshow

The ingredients for a successful slideshow are photos, photos, and more photos (with perhaps a dash of audio thrown in, which I'll address later in the chapter).

To create a slideshow:

◆ Click the Add button and choose Add Slideshow, or choose Add Slideshow from the Project menu (or press Command-L). A new empty slideshow appears in the menu (**Figure 21.1**).

◆ Drag two or more pictures from the Media pane or the Finder to the main window (if you drag only one, then the photo is used as the background image). A new slideshow titled "My Slideshow" is created containing those pictures.

◆ Drag an iPhoto album from the Media pane to the main window (**Figure 21.2**). The slideshow that is created takes the name of the album.

To set the slideshow icon:

1. Click a slideshow to select it. A Thumbnail slider appears. If the Inspector is visible, the slider is located in the Button Info window. (This feature works only in themes where buttons include icons.)

2. Drag the Thumbnail slider to choose one of the slideshow's photos (**Figure 21.3**).

3. Click outside the icon to deselect it and apply the change.

To delete a slideshow:

◆ If you want to remove a slideshow, click its button in the main window and press Delete or choose Delete from the Edit menu.

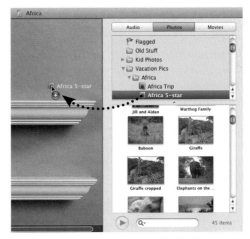

Figure 21.1 When you create an empty slideshow, it appears as a new button in the menu.

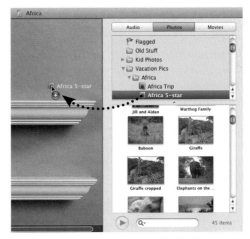

Figure 21.2 Drag an iPhoto album from the Media pane to the menu to create a slideshow containing all of the album's pictures.

Figure 21.3 The Slideshow slider lets you pick a photo to use as the button's icon.

Figure 21.4 When you add photos to the AutoPlay well, the slideshow begins when the disc starts playing.

Figure 21.5 Crop photos in iPhoto to the 4 x 3 (DVD) constraint before importing them into iDVD.

iDVD as Presenter

You can use an iDVD slideshow as a presentation tool. Create your presentation in Keynote or PowerPoint, then save each slide as a PDF file. Import those files into iDVD as a slideshow. This puts your presentation on the same disc as other multimedia materials (videos, etc.), which can be played back on any DVD player, not just a computer. At the very least, you'll have a backup of your presentation in case your original file is lost or damaged.

✔ Tips

■ iDVD now has the capability to include movies in a slideshow. Simply drag one to the Slideshow Editor (see the next page).

■ You can also drag photos or albums directly from the iPhoto application to iDVD's menu to create a new slideshow. That applies to folders containing images in the Finder, too.

■ Use the left or right arrow key to view the slideshow icon photos one by one, or if you don't want to drag the slider with the mouse.

■ If you want a slideshow to start as soon as you insert a DVD disc into a player, switch to the Map view and drag your photos to the AutoPlay well (**Figure 21.4**). Double-clicking the well with photos added brings up the AutoPlay Slideshow editor, which features the same options described throughout the rest of this chapter.

■ To ensure that your photos display correctly in iDVD, crop them first in iPhoto. Select the photo and click the Edit button to enter Edit mode, then click the Crop button. Choose 4 x 3 (DVD) from the Constrain popup menu (**Figure 21.5**). If your project is widescreen, choose 16 x 9 (HD). Move or resize the selection box so that the image appears as you'd like it to, then click the Apply button. When you bring it into iDVD, it will have the proper size ratio.

■ An iDVD slideshow displays its photos as static images. If you want to add some movement to them, use the Ken Burns Effect in iMovie or iPhoto and create a movie that contains just the photos you'd use in a slideshow (see Chapter 11). Then, import that movie file as a regular movie. (It's not actually a slideshow in iDVD's eyes, but you get the same overall effect.)

Setting Slideshow Options

Now that you've created a slideshow, use the Slideshow editor to change several settings that pertain to how long each photo appears, whether the slideshow repeats, and more.

To enter the Slideshow editor:

◆ Double-click a slideshow in the menu (or in the Map view) to bring up the Slideshow editor (**Figure 21.6**).

To set the slide duration:

◆ Choose a time from the Slide Duration popup menu to specify how long each photo remains onscreen before loading the next one (**Figure 21.7**).

If you've included background audio in your slideshow (see "Adding Background Audio," later in this chapter), you can also choose Fit To Audio, which divides the total audio playing time by the number of photos to come up with an equal display time for each photo (for example, a slideshow of five photos that contains 60 seconds of audio would display each picture for 12 seconds).

The last option, Manual, requires the viewer to advance the frames using the DVD player's controls. Manual is not available if you add background audio.

To set the transition style:

◆ Choose a transition type from the Transition popup menu (**Figure 21.8**). As with transitions between menus (see Chapter 18), this setting applies only when you're advancing to the next slide; if you switch to the previous image, no transition occurs.

For transitions that can operate in different directions, such as Cube, click a directional arrow to the right of the popup menu.

Figure 21.6 The Slideshow editor contains the options you need to control your slideshow.

Figure 21.7 The Slide Duration popup menu controls how long a photo appears onscreen before advancing.

Figure 21.8 Click the Transition popup menu to choose an effect that plays each time the slide advances.

If you don't see titles and comments, enable them in iDVD's Slideshow preferences.

Figure 21.9 Click to type a title and comment for the slide.

Figure 21.10 The Settings dialog provides a few miscellaneous options.

Figure 21.11 The navigation arrows that appear are strictly visual aids. Clicking them serves only to make your index finger sore.

To edit titles and comments:

◆ iDVD copies each photo's title and comments from iPhoto. If you plan to make these visible, click the title or comment area below a photo and type your title and comments (**Figure 21.9**).

To apply miscellaneous settings:

1. Click the Settings button to display the Settings dialog (**Figure 21.10**).

2. Enable or disable the following options:

   ▲ **Loop slideshow** makes the show repeat once it reaches the last photo. Your viewers will need to return to the menu using their player's controls.

   ▲ **Display navigation arrows** shows a pair of arrows onscreen that indicate more photos are available before and after the current one (**Figure 21.11**). These arrows are just decoration; they aren't buttons that can be clicked to advance the slideshow.

   ▲ **Add image files to DVD-ROM** includes copies of the image files on the disc so that anyone with a computer can access them (see "Adding DVD-ROM Data" in Chapter 18).

   ▲ **Show titles and comments** displays the photos' text in the Slideshow editor and during the slideshow.

   ▲ **Duck audio while playing movies** reduces the volume of background music If your slideshow contains a movie file, the last option reduces the volume of background music so it doesn't compete with the audio from the movie.

To preview the slideshow:

◆ With the Slideshow editor open, click the Preview button. You can also go back to the menu, preview the project from there, and then click the slideshow's icon, but previewing from within the Slideshow editor is easier.

To remove photos from a slideshow:

1. Select one or more photos in the Slideshow editor.

2. Press Delete, or choose Delete from the Edit menu.

To exit the Slideshow editor:

◆ Click the Return button to go back to the menu.

✔ Tips

■ You can choose to always include high-resolution slideshow photos on the DVD-ROM portion of your disc. Open iDVD's preferences, click the Slideshow icon, and enable Always add original slideshow photos to DVD-ROM contents.

■ Does a thick black band appear around your photos when you preview the slide-show? iDVD shrinks the images to fit within the TV Safe Area. To turn off this feature (if you're going to view the DVD on a computer, for example), open iDVD's preferences and click the Slideshow icon. Then, disable the option marked Always scale slides to TV Safe area (**Figure 21.12**).

■ Click the list style buttons at the upper-right corner of the Slideshow editor to switch between viewing just thumbnails of your images and viewing them in a list with filenames and comments displayed (**Figure 21.13**).

Figure 21.12 Images are usually scaled to fit within the TV Safe Area, but you can turn off this option. Compare this example with the same slide on the previous page.

List style buttons

Figure 21.13 Photos can be viewed in a list, too.

A Pointer about Pointers

When you add a photo from the Media pane, iDVD creates a pointer to the photo's original image file; it doesn't store a new copy. So, if you add a photo to your slide-show, then edit it in iPhoto later (such as cropping it or converting it to black and white), the edited version appears in your slideshow.

This also explains why, if you edit a photo in iPhoto, that picture's thumbnail image isn't updated in your slideshow, even if the correct version appears when you preview the slideshow. iDVD creates a thumbnail image of the photo when it's added to the slideshow.

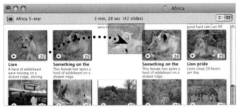

Figure 21.14 Add one or more photos from the Media pane by dragging them to the Slideshow editor.

Figure 21.15 Drag one or more photos to a new location in the Slideshow editor to rearrange them.

Before slides arranged   *After slides arranged*

Figure 21.16 The slideshow icon is based on the photo positions within the slideshow. If you've chosen the photo in the number 2 position as the icon (left), and then move a different photo to that position, the new photo becomes the icon (right).

Adding Photos

I never seem to hit upon the right combination of photos when I create a slideshow—there's always one (or two, or twenty) more that *really must* go in. iDVD has a limit of 9,801 photos—but it's hard to really call that a *limit*.

To add photos to the slideshow:

1. Double-click a slideshow to enter the Slideshow editor (if it's not already open).

2. Drag one or more image files from the Media pane or the Finder to the Slideshow editor (**Figure 21.14**).

To rearrange photos:

◆ Drag one or more images to a new location within the Slideshow editor. The other images are re-ordered to accommodate the change (**Figure 21.15**).

✔ Tips

■ Don't drag new photos to the slideshow's icon in the menu—they'll change the icon, but won't be added to the slideshow. (See "Using Motion" in Chapter 19.) Make sure you're adding them to the Slideshow editor.

■ Rearranging the order of the photos changes the preview icon for your slideshow in the menu (**Figure 21.16**). For example, if the icon is photo number 2 and you move another picture into the number 2 position in the Slideshow editor, the latter photo appears as the icon when you return to the menu.

■ You can add multiple copies of the same photo to a slideshow, in the event that you want an image to repeat later.

ADDING PHOTOS

Adding Background Audio

Just as audio can play in the background of a menu, slideshows can include audio, too.

To add background audio:

1. Double-click a slideshow to enter the Slideshow editor (if it's not already open).

2. Drag one or more audio files, or an iTunes playlist, from the Media pane to the Audio well (**Figure 21.17**). You can also drag audio files from the Finder.

   When you add audio to the well, the Slide Duration popup menu automatically switches to Fit To Audio, which divides the total audio playing time by the number of photos to come up with an equal display time for each photo.

To set the audio volume:

◆ Drag the Slideshow volume slider to control how loud or soft your background music plays (**Figure 21.18**).

To remove background audio:

◆ In the Slideshow editor, drag the music file out of the Audio well. A gray speaker icon indicates that no audio is set.

✔ Tips

■ You can also drag QuickTime movies to the Audio well; iDVD ignores the video track and plays the audio.

■ Need some visual entertainment in the background at your next party (gotta use that obnoxiously huge widescreen television for something, right)? Load up a slideshow with your favorite images and drag an iTunes playlist to the Audio well. If it's an exceptionally long party, enable the Loop slideshow option. Burn the disc, pop it into your DVD player, and then go mix some martinis!

Figure 21.17 Drag one or more songs from the Media pane to the Audio well to add background audio.

Figure 21.18 iDVD assumes you want softer music behind your slideshow, and sets the Slideshow volume slider to half the maximum volume.

Keep 'Em Entertained

Remember in Chapter 10 when I advised you to trim your footage so that your audience wouldn't get bored? The same applies to slideshows. I know, it's so easy to just drag virtual stacks of photos to iDVD—there's plenty of space on the disc, and it's quicker than sorting through them. Resist that urge: Add only the good shots and don't flirt with the limits of your viewers' attentions.

ADDING BACKGROUND AUDIO

Archiving, Encoding, and Burning

iMovie's purpose is to create a movie, which can be published to a Web page, sent to an iPod or Apple TV, or distributed in other ways. iDVD's purpose, however, is to create a project that can be burned to a DVD disc. It contains high-quality video and audio that will play on a consumer DVD player. Without the disc-burning step, iDVD is pretty much just an interesting exercise in customizing a user interface.

True to form, the process of burning a disc is simple: click the glowing Burn button, insert a recordable DVD disc (DVD-R, DVD-RW, DVD+R, or DVD+RW), and go outside to enjoy the sunshine for a few hours. But getting to that point, while not difficult, involves a few choices that determine the amount of data that can be stored on the disc and the quality of the finished project.

Creating a Project Archive

Burning a DVD takes a lot of hard disk space and processing power. Some people choose to build a project using one Mac (such as a laptop), and then burn the DVD on another computer (such as a desktop Mac, which boasts a faster processor). Or, perhaps your Mac doesn't include a SuperDrive. In these situations, create an archive of your project that can be copied to another machine.

If you're planning to burn a disc on your computer but don't need an archive, skip ahead to "Choosing an Encoding Setting."

To create a project archive:

1. Choose Archive Project from the File menu. If your project isn't saved, iDVD asks you to save it. To continue, click OK in the dialog that appears; otherwise, click Cancel.

2. In the Save As dialog that appears, choose a location for the archive and, optionally, change its name (**Figure 22.1**).

3. Enable or disable the following options. The estimated size of the archive appears to the right and changes based on your choices.

   ▲ **Include themes.** If your project uses themes that aren't likely to be on another computer (such as third-party themes you purchased, or favorite themes you designed), enable this option to copy the necessary information to the archive. If you leave this disabled, but your project contains custom elements, an error dialog appears on the other computer when you open the archive (**Figure 22.2**).

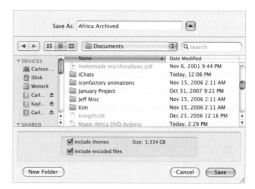

Figure 22.1 When you save your project as an archive, the Save As dialog contains archive-specific options.

Figure 22.2 Choose Include themes when saving an archive to avoid an error dialog like this one.

External Burners

For most of iDVD's existence, the only official way to burn a DVD was to do it on a Mac that contained an Apple-supplied internal SuperDrive. Now, at long last, that restriction is history: you can burn to external DVD burners directly from iDVD.

Figure 22.3 If you have protected audio files in your project, you need to authorize the computer with your iTunes Music Store ID and password.

Name ▲	Size
Africa Archived.dvdproj	4.43 GB
Africa.dvdproj	204.4 MB

Figure 22.4 An archive is significantly larger than an iDVD project file because it stores all of the media, rather than including just pointers to the data.

▲ **Include encoded files.** iDVD can encode material in the background, which reduces the time it takes to burn the disc (see "Choosing an Encoding Setting" on the next page). Including these files means it will take less time to burn the project on another machine, but it also makes the archive size larger.

4. Click Save. After a few minutes, depending on the size of your project, a new archive file is created.

✔ Tips

■ An archive contains all the data your project needs—except fonts. If your project contains a font that may not be on the computer to which you're sending the archive, be sure to also send a copy of the font.

■ If you've included any protected audio files (such as songs purchased from the iTunes Music Store) in your archive, you won't be able to open the project on another computer unless that machine is authorized by you. A warning dialog appears (**Figure 22.3**), and then opens iTunes so you can input your iTunes Music Store identification and password.

■ So why not just copy the project file? To save disk space while you're working, iDVD includes pointers to the media and other data in your project, not the data itself. Copying just the project file to another machine wouldn't include that information. An archive packs it all into a nice tidy package (**Figure 22.4**).

CREATING A PROJECT ARCHIVE

Choosing an Encoding Setting

iDVD employs three encoding methods: Best Performance, High Quality, and Professional Quality.

To choose an encoding setting for the current project:

1. Choose Project Info from the Project menu or press Command-I.

2. Choose an option from the Encoding popup menu (**Figure 22.5**).

To choose an encoding setting for new projects:

1. Open iDVD's preferences and click the Projects icon.

2. For the Encoding setting, click the radio button beside the type of encoding you wish to use.

Best Performance

Best Performance provides up to 60 minutes of video and shorter burn times than High Quality. iDVD encodes the video while it's running, whether you're doing something else in iDVD or working in another program (**Figure 22.6**).

High Quality

If your project exceeds 60 minutes, or you want to make sure you're getting a higher quality encoding than Best Performance, use the High Quality mode. After you start the burn process, iDVD examines the video to determine where it can apply different levels of compression (a process called Variable Bitrate, or VBR, encoding).

Figure 22.5 The encoding options are located in the Project Info window, as well as in iDVD's preferences.

Figure 22.6 With the Best Performance setting enabled, iDVD encodes movies in the background. The Project Info window reports on the progress.

Figure 22.7 Professional Quality projects tend to producer richer color fidelity.

Encoding and Burn Times

To give you a rough idea of how long it takes for iDVD to encode projects using the encoding settings, here are the results of burning a two-hour project on a 2.4 GHz iMac.

High Quality: 1 hours 15 minutes.
Professional Quality: 3 hours 52 minutes.

High Quality

Best Performance

High Quality

Best Performance

Figure 22.8 These examples come from a 118-minute project (High Quality) and the same footage in a 48-minute project (Best Performance). More motion and noise gets more compression (top), resulting in pixelation around the trees (detail). However, when there is less motion, the two encoding styles look very much alike (bottom, with detail).

Professional Quality

Professional Quality uses the same encoding algorithms found in Apple's pro-level applications. Like High Quality, it uses VBR, but it takes two passes through the footage to optimize the compression. Professional Quality projects tend to feature richer colors and better reproduction than High Quality projects (**Figure 22.7**).

✔ Tips

- If you're using Best Performance, wait until the assets are finished encoding in the Project Info window before you burn.

- High and Professional Quality do not encode video in the background the way Best Performance does. Instead, they perform calculations during the burning phase. So, don't stare at the Encoding area waiting for the encoding to finish, because it hasn't started.

- As projects get longer than 60 minutes, their image quality is more likely to decrease due to the additional compression that needs to be applied. If higher image quality is important to you, try not to skirt that two-hour border with your project sizes (**Figure 22.8**).

- After you burn a project using High or Professional Quality, iDVD holds onto the files it encoded. However, if you remove any assets from the project and want to burn it again, be sure to first choose Delete Encoded Assets from the Advanced menu to force iDVD to re-scan the footage and choose the best compression settings.

- The Capacity figure in the Project Info window is based on the type of encoding you've specified. If iDVD is set to use Best Performance but the capacity exceeds 4.2 GB, switch to High or Professional Quality—iDVD changes its estimate.

Burning the DVD

Before you click the Burn button, make sure you have enough hard disk space available: at least twice the amount the project occupies. You can view your project's size and the free space on the hard disk that contains your project by choosing Project Info from the Project menu.

Figure 22.9 In the Project Info window, change the name of the disc when it's inserted in a computer.

To change the name of the burned disc:

1. Choose Project Info from the Project menu, or press Command-I. The Project Info window appears (**Figure 22.9**).

2. Type a new name in the Disc Name field. After the disc is burned, this name is used when the DVD is mounted on a computer's desktop.

3. Close the window to apply the change.

Figure 22.10 Use the Project Info window to locate missing assets.

To locate a missing asset:

1. Choose Project Info from the Project menu, or press Command-I to display the Project Info window.

2. Scroll through the asset list to find entries with a zero (0) in the Status column (**Figure 22.10**).

3. Double-click the missing asset to bring up the Missing Files dialog.

4. Select a file in the dialog and click the Find File button.

5. Locate the file and press OK. The Status column displays a checkmark. Note that for missing imported videos, you need to re-link the video and audio portions (just point to the same file).

6. Click OK to exit the dialog.

How to Fix Missing Assets

The Project Info dialog tracks everything you've added to the project, even assets that you've deleted. If the file cannot be found, iDVD will not proceed when the time comes to burn.

I learned this the hard way when I dragged a JPEG image file to a menu background, decided it didn't look good, and then deleted it from the Background well in the Menu pane. Since the image no longer appeared in the project, I deleted it from my hard disk.

There are two solutions:

◆ Double-click the item in the Project Info window and choose another image.

◆ Go to the Map view and delete the asset entirely.

Normal *Activated*

Figure 22.11 You need to click the Burn button only once to start the process (some earlier versions required two clicks). So, really, there's no good reason to hide the button behind the safety iris—except that it's cool.

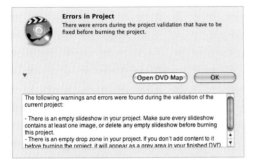

Figure 22.12 If errors are found before burning, iDVD gives you the opportunity to fix or ignore them.

In the Map view, position your mouse pointer over a warning icon to locate potential burn problems.

Figure 22.13 The disc burning process goes through five stages of encoding and writing data to disc. The small preview helps you determine how far along the process has advanced.

To burn the DVD:

1. Click the Burn button; the iris reveals the glowing Burn button that's been hiding under iDVD's interface (**Figure 22.11**).

   If any assets are missing, iDVD displays a warning dialog (**Figure 22.12**). The Map view also displays potential burn problems.

   (The "closed" Burn button is like the bright red safety cover that's always mounted over The Big Important Button—the one that launches the missiles, opens the airlocks, or initiates the self-destruct sequence that destroys the villian's secret underground lair in all those movies.)

   Otherwise, the program asks you to insert a blank recordable DVD disc.

2. A progress dialog appears that identifies the stages of the process (**Figure 22.13**):

   ▲ **Stage 1: Prepare.** iDVD ensures that it has everything it needs to continue burning.

   ▲ **Stage 2: Process Menus.** Buttons, motion menus, and other menu interface elements are rendered and encoded.

   ▲ **Stage 3: Process Slideshows.** Slideshow photos are resized and compressed as needed. If you've specified slideshow transitions, they are rendered separately during this stage.

   ▲ **Stage 4: Process Movies.** Depending on which encoding method you've chosen, this stage usually takes the longest.

   ▲ **Stage 5: Burn.** The footage is *multiplexed*, which combines the audio and video data into a single stream that can be read by DVD players. Burning is when the laser actually etches your data into the surface of the disc.

BURNING THE DVD

✔ Tips

- If you've specified Best Performance, wait for asset encoding to finish before starting the burn process.

- Remember that the total space occupied on the disc includes motion menus, slideshows, etc. So if your movie is 56 minutes long, you may still get an error message that the project is too big.

- Earlier versions of iDVD required you to enable the Motion button to include motion on the disc, but iDVD now renders the motion elements whether the Motion button is highlighted or not. To burn a project with no motion, set the Loop Duration slider in the Menu Info window to zero (00:00).

- I frequently burn test copies of a project to a rewriteable DVD-RW disc, so I'm not throwing away a bunch of shiny platters. When you insert such a disc that already has data on it, iDVD gives you the option to erase it before continuing with the burn process (**Figure 22.14**).

- Including transitions between menus or within slideshows adds time to the burning process.

- Did you create a widescreen movie in iMovie, but it's not appearing as widescreen in your DVD player? Check to see if the player has a 16:9 or letterbox feature...some models (such as mine at home) play the movie full frame if it doesn't detect a flag on the disc instructing it to letterbox the picture.

- Wondering at what speed your Super-Drive is burning the disc? The answer is found in Mac OS X's console.log file. After you burn a project, open the file, located at [Computer]/Library/Logs/Console/.

Figure 22.14 If you insert a rewriteable disc that contains data, iDVD can erase it during the burn stage.

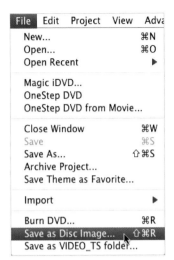

Figure 22.15 "Burn" a disc image to your hard drive.

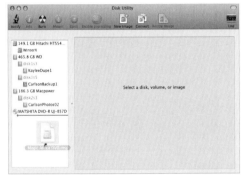

Figure 22.16 Drag a disc image to Disk Utility to burn its contents to a DVD disc.

Save as VIDEO_TS Folder

If you just want to test the quality of the encoded material on the same machine, choose Save as VIDEO_TS folder from the File menu. This option does the same work as creating a disc image, but the files are just stored in a folder (and therefore are not as transportable). Point DVD Player at that folder to watch the "disc."

Saving as a Disc Image

Until iDVD 5, you needed to own a Mac with an Apple-supplied SuperDrive to burn iDVD projects. It wouldn't work with third-party external burners.

Now, that restriction is gone. However, there are still occasions when you want to save the project as a disc image, which effectively "burns" your project to the hard drive. For example, you may want to burn a DVD disc from that disc image on another computer, or mount the image on your desktop and preview the final project using the DVD Player application.

To save as a disc image:

1. Instead of clicking the Burn button, choose Save As Disc Image from the File menu, or press Command-Shift-R (**Figure 22.15**).

2. Choose a location on your hard disk to save the disc image; make sure you have plenty of free space.

3. Click the Save button. iDVD follows the same procedure as when it burns a disc.

To burn a DVD disc from a disc image:

1. Launch Disk Utility (located in Applications > Utilities).

2. Drag the disc image from the Finder to the left-hand column (**Figure 22.16**); or, choose Open from the Images menu.

3. Select the disc image in Disk Utility and click the Burn button.

4. Insert a recordable disc.

To play a disc image using DVD Player:

1. Double-click the disc image to mount the disc as if it were a physical DVD.

2. Launch the DVD Player application.

After the Burn

When the burning process is complete, iDVD spits out the DVD disc and asks if you'd like to make another copy (**Figure 22.17**). If so, insert a new disc; otherwise, click Done.

Here are a few other suggested things to do while you're in your cooling down period.

Test your project

Just because you have a shiny disc in hand doesn't guarantee that it works. Test it on your own machine using DVD Player. Test it on friends' Macs and PCs, and insert it in your consumer DVD player. Test, test, test, or you may find yourself singing, "To every season, burn, burn, burn...".

Delete encoded assets

If you don't need to burn another disc, you can free up some hard disk space by deleting the project's encoded assets, which are stored in the project file.

Create an archive of the project for offline storage to make sure you have all of the original footage.

To delete encoded assets:

◆ From the Advanced menu, choose Delete Encoded Assets.

Make duplicates

If you want to make copies of the DVD without going through the iDVD burning process, use Disk Utility or other software such as Roxio's Toast (www.roxio.com).

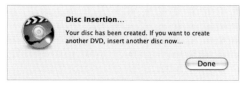

Figure 22.17 If you're creating multiple copies of the same disc, burn them in succession so you don't have to go through the encoding stage each time.

TROUBLESHOOTING

Software is never perfect, and unfortunately iMovie 3 had more than its fair share of "challenges," as an optimistic friend of mine likes to say. iMovie versions 4 through 6 were improved, but still suffered some glitches. In that respect, maybe it's best that iMovie '08 is a completely rewritten application. Although it's still new, it seems to be a bit more robust than what we've become accustomed to (though there are always exceptions).

My first bit of troubleshooting advice is to make sure you're running the latest versions of iMovie and iDVD; check the iLife page at Apple's Web site (`www.apple.com/ilife/`) or run Software Update (in your System Preferences or from the Apple menu).

Also, check Apple's online support discussion forums for iMovie and iDVD (`discussions. info.apple.com`) to see if other users have found solutions or workarounds to a problem you may be experiencing. And check some of the resources in Appendix B for up-to-the-minute reports and troubleshooting. I owe a great debt to many folks online who have prodded the programs to find answers.

Finally—and perhaps most important—*give Apple feedback* (`www.apple.com/feedback`). It's the best way to communicate what needs fixing (and yes, the developers do listen).

iMovie and iDVD Troubleshooting

iMovie seems to prefer lots of memory and fast processors, but even on powerful Macs you might see sluggish behavior. Try the following suggestions to improve performance.

Make the iMovie window smaller

Use the resize handle on the bottom-right corner of the iMovie window to make it as small as it will go.

Quit other running applications

This frees up more memory for iMovie to use. Although Mac OS X manages memory better than Mac OS 9, I've seen iMovie and iDVD gain some pep if they're not competing with other processes.

Defragment your hard disk

You can run into performance issues if your hard disk space is severely fragmented—there aren't enough open stretches of disk space available to write entire files, so the files are broken up into pieces to fit the available free locations.

The best way to defragment a disk is to make a complete backup copy of it, erase the drive, and then restore the data.

Turn off FileVault

FileVault is a technology introduced in Mac OS X 10.3 that creates an encrypted version of your Home directory. However, iDVD and iMovie store their project files in the Home directory, which means that when FileVault is active, the computer is constantly encrypting and decrypting massive quantities of data on the fly. Turn it off in Mac OS X's Security preference pane.

Trash iMovie or iDVD preferences

If the program's preferences get corrupted, it places a load on the program's operation. iMovie and iDVD re-create the files they need the next time you launch the program.

To trash iMovie or iDVD preferences:

1. Quit the application. (You may want to quit all running applications, too.)

2. Go to your preferences folder at [Home]/Library/Preferences/, and delete the following files (you may not have all of the iMovie files):

    ▲ iMovie Preferences

    ▲ com.apple.imovie.plist

    ▲ com.apple.iMovie7.plist

    ▲ com.apple.iDVD.plist

Fixing out of sync audio/video

If your audio and video are out of sync in a video clip, make sure your audio was recorded at 16-bit, not 12-bit. See the following article for more information: http://docs.info.apple.com/article.html?artnum=61636.

Consult Apple's support pages

Apple publishes technotes about common issues and workarounds: www.apple.com/support/imovie/ and www.apple.com/support/idvd/.

Disc Burning

Here are some things to check if your discs are turning into drink coasters (or if you're not even getting to the burn stage).

Have lots of disk space

Make sure you have plenty of hard disk space available. Figure at least twice the size of your iDVD project as being a good starting point. You may have to copy your project to another disk (such as an external FireWire drive) and run it from there; iDVD stores its working files and encoded media within the project file, so even if you have a drive with lots of free space, iDVD will ignore it if the project file is not located there.

Ensure disk is formatted correctly

If you're using an external drive, make sure it's formatted as a Mac OS Extended (Journaled) volume. Some drives are pre-formatted for Windows or Unix operating systems, and although the Mac can read and write to them, iMovie and iDVD need to use Mac OS Extended (Journaled). Use Disk Utility to erase and reformat the drive.

Delete encoded assets

Some previously-encoded material could be causing problems. From iDVD's Advanced menu, choose Delete Encoded Assets, which deletes any rendered footage and forces iDVD to re-encode the material from scratch.

Check DVD media

Unfortunately, sometimes the problem is the blank DVD disc you're trying to burn onto. This can happen with less expensive discs purchased in bulk, but has been known to affect reputable manufacturers' discs, too. If you're getting errors, try a new media brand.

Clean your SuperDrive

A tiny laser burns pits into a disc, resulting in data that a computer or DVD player can read. If your SuperDrive has accumulated dust, it can throw off the beam and ruin your burn. Spray a little compressed air into the slot (but don't go crazy with it).

Set Energy Saver settings

Disc burning is processor-intensive. Go to the Energy Saver preference pane in Mac OS X's System Preferences and set the processor performance to Highest and the hard drive to never spin down. Also make sure that the computer won't go to sleep after a period of inactivity.

Burn during the day

It's convenient to start a burn late at night so the process will complete while you're sleeping. However, Mac OS X performs some nightly system maintenance at approximately 3 a.m., which can interfere with burn performance. Burn your project during the day to see if this is the culprit.

Change audio quality

iMovie and iDVD use audio set to 48.000 kHz (16-bit). However, some audio sources may record at 44.100 kHz, which has been known to cause burning problems.

To change a movie's audio quality:

1. Export your movie from iMovie to a QuickTime file using Expert Settings.

2. In the Movie Settings dialog, under Sound options, click the Settings button.

3. Click the Rate popup menu and choose 48.000.

4. Export the clip, then import it into iDVD.

RESOURCES

Essential Information

***iMovie & iDVD: Visual QuickStart Guide* companion Web site**

http://www.jeffcarlson.com/imovievqs/

Apple iLife

http://www.apple.com/ilife/

Canon Digital Camcorders

http://www.canondv.com/

Sony Digital Camcorders

http://www.sonystyle.com/

JVC Digital Camcorders

http://www.jvc.com/

Panasonic Digital Camcorders

http://www.panasonic.com/

Recommended Books

Real World Digital Video, 2nd Edition,
Pete Shaner and Gerald Everett Jones
(Peachpit Press, 2004)

*Take Control of Making Music with
GarageBand* and *Take Control of
Recording with GarageBand*, Jeff Tolbert
(TidBITS Electronic Publishing, 2006)

http://www.takecontrolbooks.com/

*Killer Camera Rigs that You Can
Build*, by Dan Selakovich (Angel Dog
Entertainment, 2004)

http://www.dvcamerarigs.com/

*Behind the Seen: How Walter Murch
Edited Cold Mountain using Final Cut
Pro and What This Means for Cinema*,
by Charles Koppelman (Peachpit Press,
2004)

http://www.peachpit.com/

Online Tutorials and Reference

HD for Indies Weblog

http://www.hdforindies.com/

The "Unofficial" iMovie FAQ

http://www.danslagle.com/mac/iMovie/

Film Underground

http://www.cyberfilmschool.com/

DVcreators.net

http://www.dvcreators.net/

2-pop.com

http://www.2-pop.com/

Post Forum

http://www.postforum.com/

Audio Editing Applications

SoundStudio

http://www.freeverse.com/soundstudio/

SndSampler

http://www.sndsampler.com/

Fission

http://www.rogueamoeba.com/fission/

iDVD Themes

iDVD ThemePak

http://www.idvdthemepak.com/

Other iMovie-Related Software

Still Life

http://www.grantedsw.com/still-life/

Photo to Movie

http://www.lqgraphics.com/

Royalty-Free Audio Clips

Freeplay Music

http://www.freeplaymusic.com/

Killersound

http://www.killersound.com/

Sound Dogs

http://www.sounddogs.com/

SmartSound

http://www.smartsound.com/

INDEX

INDEX

INDEX

INDEX

Y

YouTube, 59, 64

Z

zooming. *See also* Ken Burns Effect
   basics of, 33
   depth of field and, 26
   digital zoom feature, 14
   vs. dollying, 34

23. Sept 08

Amazon

22.42

103645